The Comfort of Crows

Also by Margaret Renkl

Late Migrations:
A Natural History of
Love and Loss

Graceland, At Last:
Notes on Hope and Heartache
From the American South

The

Comfort

of

Crows

A Backyard Year

Margaret Renkl

Art by Billy Renkl

Spiegel and Grau

S&G

Spiegel & Grau, New York
www.spiegelandgrau.com

Jacket design by Charlotte Strick; photograph of jacket art by Amir Aghareb
Interior design by Meighan Cavanaugh

Library of Congress Cataloging-in-Publication Data Available Upon Request

ISBN 978-1-954118-46-1 (hardcover)
ISBN 978-1-954118-50-8 (eBook)

Printed in Canada
The Comfort of Crows is FSC certified. It is printed on chlorine-free paper made with 30% post-consumer waste. It uses only vegetable- and soy-based ink.

First Edition
10   9   8   7   6   5   4   3   2

For my children,

who give me faith in the future

Contents

Wherever You Are, Stop What You're Doing ...... *xv*

Winter

❧

The Season of Sleeping *1*

   Praise Song for the Coming Budburst *3*

First Bird *5*

How to Catch a Fox *9*

The Bird Feeder *15*

The Winter Garden *19*

   Praise Song for the Praise Song of a
   Song Sparrow in Winter *23*

Hate to See That Evening Sun Go Down *25*

A Seed in Darkest Winter *29*

   Praise Song for the Dog's Marvelous Nose .. *33*

Done with Waiting *35*

It's a Mystery *39*

   Praise Song for Mole Hands in Coyote Scat .. *43*

The Crow Family *45*

The Knothole *51*

Wild Joy *55*

Ephemeral *59*

   Praise Song for a Spring I Was Not
   Alive to See *63*

Spring

❧

The Season of Waking 65

Who Will Mourn Them When
They Are Gone? 67

*Praise Song for the Maple Tree's
First Green* 71

The Names of Flowers 73

The Beautiful World beside the Broken One ... 77

Wildflowers at My Feet and Songbirds
in My Trees 81

*Praise Song for the Killdeer on the
School Softball Field* 85

Metamorphosis 87

*Praise Song for the Alien in
the Shade Garden* 93

Hide and Seek 95

My Life in Mice 99

*Praise Song for the Redbird Who
Has Lost His Crest and the Skink
Who Has Lost His Tail* 105

The Bobcat Next Door 107

And Then There Were None 111

Dust to Dust 115

Praise Song for Solomon's Seal 119

An Acolyte of Benign Neglect 121

Praise Song for All the Beginnings 125

The Grief of Lost Time 127

Praise Song for the Baby Chickadees 131

Summer

The Season of Singing 133

    Praise Song for the Skink Who Has
    Gone to Ground 135

Thirty-Four Is Tadpoles 137

    Praise Song for the Red Fox, Screaming
    in the Driveway 143

Loving the Unloved Animals 145

Pickers 149

Of Berries and Death 153

The Teeming Season 157

    Praise Song for the Carpenter Bees
    Eating Our Fence to Ruin 159

Kept Safe in the Womb of the World 161

Reverse Nesting 165

The Spider in My Life 171

    Praise Song for What Hides in
    Plain Sight 175

My Life in Rabbits 177

    Praise Song for the First Red Leaf
    of the Black Gum Tree 181

Dislocation 183

    Praise Song for the Ragged Season 187

The World Is a Collage 189

    Praise Song for the Holes in
    Pawpaw Leaves 193

Imagination 195

    Praise Song for Fingers That Do
    Not Form a Fist 197

Fall

✤

The Season of Making Ready ... 199

Praise Song for a Clothesline in Drought ... 201

Autumn Light ... 203

Flower of Dreams ... 207

Praise Song for the Back Side of the Sign ... 211

The Last Hummingbird ... 213

The Butterfly Cage ... 217

Praise Song for Sleeping Bees ... 221

Holiness ... 223

Praise Song for Forgetfulness ... 227

Because I Can't Stop Drinking in the Light ... 229

The Lazarus Snail ... 233

Praise Song for a Larger Home ... 239

How to Rake Leaves on a Windy Day ... 241

The Mast Year ... 245

And Now the Light Is Failing ... 251

Praise Song for Dead Leaves ... 255

Ode to a Dark Season ... 257

The Thing with Feathers ... 261

Author's Note ... 265
Author's Acknowledgments ... 267
Artist's Acknowledgments ... 269
About the Author ... 270
About the Artist ... 270

"Nature" is what we see—
The Hill—the Afternoon—
Squirrel—Eclipse—the Bumble bee . . .

—Emily Dickinson

To pay attention, this is our endless and
proper work.

—Mary Oliver

Wherever You Are,
Stop What You're Doing

🌱

S top and look at the tangled rootlets of the poison ivy vine
climbing the locust tree. Notice the way they twist around
each other like plaits in a golden braid, like tendrils of seaweed
washed to shore. Stop and look, but do not touch. Never, never
touch, not even in winter.

Stop and ponder the skeleton of the snakeroot plant, each twig
covered in tiny brown stars. The white petals, once embraced by
bees, have dried to powder and now dust the forest floor, but here
are the star-shaped sepals that held those fluffs of botanical celebration. Bend closer. Here and there are a few black seeds the
goldfinches neglected to glean. Only a few, but enough.

Stop and listen to the ragged-edged beech leaves, pale specters
of the winter forest. They are chattering ghosts, clattering amid
the bare branches of the other hardwoods. Wan light pours through
their evanescence and burnishes them to gleaming. Deep in the
gray, sleeping forest, whole beech trees flare up into whispering
creatures made of trembling gold.

Stop and consider the deep hollows of the persimmon's bark,
the way the tree has carved its own skin into neat rectangles of
sturdy protection. See how the lacy lichens have found purchase in

the channels, sharing space in the hollows. Tree and lichen belong to one another. Neither is causing the other any harm.

Stop and peer at the hummingbird nest, smaller than your thumb, in the crook of the farthest reach of an oak branch. Remember the whir of hummingbird wings. Remember the green flash of hummingbird light.

Stop and notice how closely the human teenagers resemble the whistling, clicking, preening starlings.

Stop and contemplate the hollow-boned ducks floating on the water like leaves. Like deadwood. Turtles, too, drift in the sunny water. See the way the bones in the turtle's webbed foot resemble the bones in the duck's webbed foot. Hold open your hand. Trace the outline of your fingers.

Stop and think for a time about kinship. Think for a long time about kinship.

The world lies before you, a lavish garden. However hobbled by waste, however fouled by graft and tainted by deception, it will always take your breath away.

We were never cast out of Eden. We merely turned from it and shut our eyes. To return and be welcomed, cleansed and redeemed, we are only obliged to look.

The Comfort of Crows

The Season of Sleeping

Winter ❧ Week 1

It was a December of crows.

—Claire Keegan, *Small Things Like These*

When I was young, I craved the expansiveness of heat, the languor of an afternoon so hot the only choice was stillness. I longed for light and color, impatient for the goldfinch to put on his yellow finery, for the hardwood trees to shiver into green.

Age has given me an internal source of warmth, and hubris has given us all a burning planet, but I still love the seasons of light and color. Only when I head outside do winter's consolations become clear. The small ground birds rustling in the leaf litter are suddenly visible. I can tell the song sparrows from the field sparrows, and the Carolina wrens from the winter wrens. The contours of the earth emerge, fold upon fold, as though I had been seeing before in only two dimensions. On the lake trail, I turn toward the belted kingfisher's rattling call, and there is the kingfisher himself, his shaggy crest scraping the blue sky from a branch high in the trees.

Nothing in nature exists as a metaphor, but human beings are reckless metaphor makers anyway, and only a fool could fail to find the lesson here. The cold roots of the sleeping trees along the streambed are even now taking in water. One day soon that water will rise and spring into the world in a rush of tight green leaves poised to unfurl. Everything that waits is also preparing itself to move.

Praise Song for
the Coming Budburst

It looks like a mistake, like something left behind as fall moved into winter. The framework for a leaf gone by, perhaps, or the false start of some living thing that never grew into itself.

It is not a mistake.

There was no error in its planning and none in its purposes.

All winter long the brown bud will sleep. While the cold crow calls into the gray sky, while the wet leaves blacken and begin their return to earth, the brown bud is waiting for its true self to unfold: a beginning that in sleep has already begun.

First Bird

Winter ❦ Week 2

This game is an inspiration to place yourself in natural circumstances that will yield a heavenly bird, blessing your year, your perspective, your imagination, your spirit. New year, first bird.

—LYANDA LYNN HAUPT, *Rare Encounters with Ordinary Birds*

According to birding tradition, the first bird you see on the first day of the new year sets the tone for your next twelve months. One year, the first bird I saw was a downy woodpecker, or possibly a hairy woodpecker—the two species look virtually identical, particularly to a person who spies her first bird of the new year before she has had her first coffee of the new year. Because I couldn't sort it out in the instant before the woodpecker got spooked and flew away, my theme bird that year was neither species of woodpecker. Instead it was a robin, the second bird I saw that morning. As the robin stood on the edge of the birdbath, watching me as I watched it, I found myself wondering if birds play a New Year's game called "First Human."

I love robins. I love the way they stand in the yard and cock their heads when it rains, turning an invisible ear toward the ground and listening for the sound of a worm moving toward the surface of the saturated soil. I love the way they flock up in winter, with the locals and their new offspring welcoming the migrators to a season-long family reunion. The way they call to one another in a kind of descending chortle as night begins to fall. The robins' song is the music of twilight.

But this year my first bird is a sharp-eyed crow, and I am thrilled. One of my favorite childhood stories is Aesop's tale of a thirsty crow who finds a pitcher with a bit of water in the bottom. The clever bird cannot reach the water at first but then begins to drop pebbles into the pitcher, one by one by one, and soon the water rises within reach. I am beguiled by the promise of a year watched over by this bold, problem-solving bird—the playful prankster, the curious collector, the tender parent, humankind's steadfast companion. Even if the terrible time comes when all the other songbirds are gone, lost to the fiery world, crows will remain among us, living on what we leave behind.

"What's the first bird you saw this morning?" I asked my father-in-law at our New Year's lunch last year. We were eating greens and black-eyed peas for good luck.

"I don't believe I've seen a bird today," he said.

Tucked up on the fourth floor of an apartment building at a time of year when it's too cold to stand on the balcony, of course he hadn't seen a bird. But the day wasn't over yet, and I told him to keep an eye out. "Look for a crow," I said. "Who wouldn't want to start the new year watched over by a crow? They're smart and brave and loyal . . ."

"They squawk a lot, too," he said.

He was laughing at me.

I am content for a bird to be only a bird, a representative of nothing. But on New Year's Day, still bleary-eyed from lack of sleep and lack of coffee, I googled my first bird's symbolic associations. I was surprised to discover that "What do crows symbolize?" auto-populates the search field just behind "What do crows eat?"

Many cultures have associated crows with death. Their uniformly black coloring, their harsh cries, their taste for roadkill—all may have contributed to that most famous of collective names among birds, a murder of crows. Crows have been observed conducting "funerals" for fallen flock mates, and this somber ritual may account for the gloomy associations, too.

But other cultures have associated the birds with intelligence and adaptability, even transformation, and these are the connections I'll rely on as the year unfolds. I have entered my sixties now, a time of change—to my body, to my family, to the way I think about my future—and I cling to the crow's promise of metamorphosis. What more could anyone ask from a new year than the promise—or just the hope—of renewal?

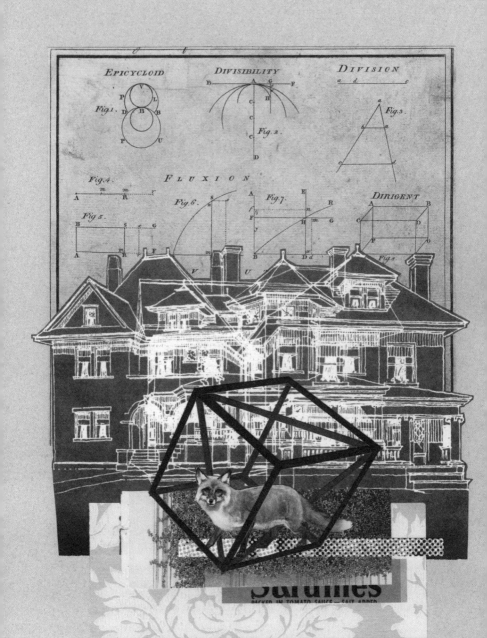

How to Catch a Fox

Winter ❧ *Week 3*

Fox had different ideas.

—CATHERINE RAVEN, *Fox & I*

The fox is sick. No question the fox is sick. At two thirty in the afternoon on an eye-squinting winter day with no leaves left on the trees to break the glare, the fox is digging next to a neighbor's mailbox, right beside the road. The fox is squinting, too, though not because of the glare. The fox's eyes are swollen into slits. It can hardly see and appears not to hear the approach of my car, not even when I pull up right beside it and roll down the window to take a picture with my phone. I watch for a while. I take many pictures. Also a video.

The fox is hungry enough to hunt in the middle of a sunny afternoon on a tightly mowed suburban lawn, but when it leaps into the air in that wonderful arcing dive that foxes have perfected for plunging headfirst into deep snow or tall grass, this fox comes up with no wiggling mouse or vole. The fox stops trying to catch whatever it hears. It sits down to scratch. The fox has mange.

More and more these days the neighborhood foxes are turning up with mange. A healthy creature with a strong immune system can fight off the mites that cause mange, but suburban foxes are struggling. The once modest little homes tucked into wild, scruffy lots here are mostly gone, replaced by giant houses in sterile yards ruthlessly landscaped to the very edge. Where are the gentle rabbits now? Where are the field mice and the voles? The prosperous new people have not learned to live peacefully with wildlife. They poison the dandelions so favored by rabbits. They poison the moles trundling under their soil and the mice skittering in their crawl spaces. A hungry fox who eats a poisoned mouse or a poisoned mole is vulnerable to the mites that cause mange.

I try to decide what to do. I keep elbow-length leather gloves and a pet carrier in the back of my car, but those are for injured turtles and orphaned opossums, needy creatures an old woman can catch. There is no chance I can catch this fox. There is also no chance the fox will survive without medical care. Mange will bring the fox a slow, terrible death.

I call the nearest wildlife rescue center to ask for help. When no one answers, I leave a message and wait with the fox, who does not know I am waiting.

The fox lies down under the trees and scratches some more. On the underside of one leg, there is an open wound that requires some licking, but mainly it is scratching. These ablutions are taking time. I wait, hoping for a call. Maybe help will come in time.

Help does not come in time. There are many sick foxes nowadays, many injured animals of every kind, and nowhere near enough wildlife rescue experts to care for all the creatures hurt by living in a world where people crowd closer and closer.

By the time the wildlife expert arrives the next morning, the fox has been gone all night, but the expert has brought a trap and teaches me how to set it. The bait is nasty—raw bacon and oily sardines and chicken parts pierced with a string. Holding my breath, I tie the raw chicken to the back of the trap. A fox with severe mange will be starving, too light to trigger the trap door, but even a starving fox will trip the trap when it tugs on the chicken.

The wildlife expert drives away. Now my job is to monitor the trap and release any creatures who are not a fox. I may or may not catch a raccoon, but I am almost certain to catch an opossum.

I will need to find a good-sized stick and a large sheet. The sheet is for when I catch the fox. A fox in a covered trap is calmer than a fox in a trap with open sides. The stick is for when I catch the opossum. A raccoon will dash away as soon as I open the trap door, but an opossum will ponder a while: *What's the rush? There's bacon here.* I need the stick to prop open the door and let the opossum leave in its own good time.

I check again and again and again, always alone to keep from frightening the sick fox should the sick fox ever reappear. At first I check every hour. Then every other hour. Finally every three hours. I am not proud of this, but I start taking the dog with me because checking this trap is taking more time than I can spare, and I might as well walk Rascal at the same time. Rascal is happy with his new walking route. Perhaps he smells the fox nearby. Probably he is just happy.

I check the trap just after sundown on the second day. I know I should check again before bedtime, but it's cold and dark, and Rascal gives me the side-eye when I pick up his leash. I decide to make the trek anyway. How sad a sick fox would be to spend the long, cold night in a trap!

I gasp when my flashlight glances across a pair of pointed ears. I drop the flashlight.

I pick up the flashlight again and shine it at the cage. The fox blinks at me but does not flinch in the light. The fox is still, impassive, a vulpine sphinx. Except for the blinking, the fox is motionless.

I consider how often a fox may have sat just this still beneath the shrubbery, watching me trudge along. I think of the fox's balletic moves, of the way its slender legs and swift, small feet are tucked beneath its body now, its bushy tail a perfect parenthesis curving around the perfect closing word.

I need to walk the half mile back to the house and fetch a sheet to cover the trap, but now Rascal has planted his own small feet in the dirt. I try to hustle him back home. Who knows what he's especially interested in—the stinky chicken? the blinking fox?— but he has decided that he is going nowhere.

I pick up the dog and drop the flashlight again. I abandon the flashlight and head home with the wiggling dog.

While Rascal struggles in my arms, I think, "That fox blinked at me."

I think, "That fox's tail is fully furred."

I think, "That fox is not sick."

Now I recall how the dirt in front of the trap had been thoroughly scraped away. The fox in the trap has an accomplice who has worked mightily to break him free.

I think, "This is a different fox."

The wildlife expert has considered the possibility that I will catch a healthy fox. He left behind a medication that prevents mange for several months, enough time to keep the healthy fox healthy until we can catch his sick companion.

"Wrap the pill in bacon and toss it into the trap," the wildlife expert tells me on the phone. "Go home. After an hour or two, check the trap again. If the bacon is gone, open the trap and send the fox on its way."

THE COMFORT OF CROWS

This is what I do, though I do not see the fox heading on its way. I am standing beside it, close enough to smell its musk, close enough to see the tips of its hair rustle just slightly with every breath of wind. I open the trap, checking my feet to be sure I am standing far enough to the side, not blocking the door, and while I am preoccupied with my feet and the machinery of trap doors, the fox vanishes. It is not a fox. It is a blur of falling leaves, red and gold. A phantom rush of wildness. A mirage of a miracle, pungent and swift.

I saw it. I did not see it. I will never see it again.

One good thing about catching the wrong fox is that you will never catch that fox again. That fox has learned about traps. Time to bait and set the trap once more. The vile sardines really aren't that bad when placed on a scale opposite a dying fox. I set the trap and walk away.

But only for a little while. I will catch the fox, or I won't, but never again will I be free to walk away forever.

The Bird Feeder

Winter ❧ *Week 4*

We have been animals all our lives.

—Maggie Smith, "Animals"

Cold weather is hard on creatures who don't hibernate. Small animals and birds are burning more calories to keep warm just as their best sources of food—seeds and berries and insects—have disappeared. Predators are burning more calories to keep warm just as their best sources of food—smaller animals and birds—have grown less plentiful, too. Many rodents and reptiles are sleeping deep underground now, and many birds have flown farther south for the winter.

Worse, when temperatures dip below freezing, drinking water is hard to come by for birds and mammals alike. To keep their feathers primed for optimal insulation, birds also need water for bathing, even in winter, and a trickle of sun-warmed ice isn't enough.

For human beings, particularly for a human being nursing a monstrous cold, it's a good time to stay indoors, to participate in the natural world by observing it through a window. Fortunately, there is hardly a window in this house that doesn't look out onto a feeder or birdbath. There's a thistle feeder just outside my office, a mealworm feeder outside our bedroom, and another mealworm feeder outside the living room. There are feeders with shelled peanuts and whole peanuts and safflower seeds and suet, all visible from my writing table in the family room. There are birdbaths of varying heights on three sides of the house, and one of them contains a heating element that keeps the water from freezing. On very cold mornings, birds of all kinds gather nearby and flutter down in waves to drink.

Some of the birds who frequent this yard in winter aren't looking for peanuts. They're looking for the thirsty creatures who come to the birdbath, for the hungry birds who come to the feeders. Because I am too sick to go out, I carry my laptop from room to room, just to vary the view. Almost every day I catch with the corner of my eye a Cooper's hawk barreling past some window in a flash of wings and yellow claws, or I notice a barred owl sitting still and silent on a tree limb. In winter it is hungry enough to hunt during daytime, too, patiently waiting for some crawling thing to stir in the brush pile, for some unwary dove to land on the ground under the safflower feeder, looking for seeds the other birds dropped.

I think of the woman I know who looked out her window one summer and saw a rat snake climbing the pole to her nest box, heading straight for the place where the baby bluebirds were trapped. Without giving any thought to the reason why bluebirds raise as many as five clutches each year, the woman ran outside with her hedge clippers and cut that poor snake in half. I have seen a rat snake in a state of fear, and I can hardly let myself remember that story, but I remember it every time I see the little hawk slamming into the hedge where the bluebirds have taken shelter just past my own window.

The only thing to do when a Cooper's hawk stakes out a feeder is to take the feeder down, much as it kills my heart to leave my avian neighbors unprovided for in this changing neighborhood where natural food sources have become so much less plentiful. The hawk and the owl must eat, too, I know, but I don't wish to make their bloody work any easier. I am drawn to their fierce wild-ness, but this is not the kind of bird feeder I had in mind. I don't know if I'm right to feel this way.

The Winter Garden

Winter ❧ Week 5

> Life can change in an instant, that's a fact. But life isn't
> changing only in those split seconds when it appears to
> change, when someone is there and then gone.
>
> —MARY LAURA PHILPOTT, *Bomb Shelter*

Back in the time when Nashville still got several snows each winter, and snow days meant sledders on the hill beyond my home-office window, I would work to the sound of children squealing with the joy of speed and freedom. One year I got a text from a parent supervising the sledding: "It's a robin migration out in your front yard. Do you put food out there for them?"

In all the years I've been putting out bird feeders, I've never seen a robin at even one of them. But our yard is always popular with these birds, especially in winter, because we don't use any poisons, and because we let the leaves lie where they fall. Sometimes a giant flock of robins and a giant flock of starlings, plus countless ground foragers—sparrows and wrens and juncos—will be out there at once, competing for space to scratch around the leafy ground, looking for overwintering insects.

It didn't surprise me to find dozens of robins in our yard on that snowy day, but it surprised me to see what they were doing. A robin's usual practice is to pick earthworms out of the exposed soil churned up by moles, but there are no worms near the surface on freezing days. Instead, these robins were eating dried berries from the monkey grass bordering our front walkway, the border my mother planted when we first bought this house nearly three decades ago. Normally my husband mows down the dead monkey grass after the first frost, but that year he hadn't gotten around to it yet. Haywood and I are desultory gardeners.

In spring I prefer planting to weeding. In summer I like to watch birds pulling seeds from dried flowers, so I let the flowers fall to ruin instead of deadheading them to force the plant to produce new blooms. In fall it has always seemed nothing less than criminal to tidy up the golden windfall of sugar maple leaves covering the ground like pirate treasure in a storybook.

In spite of these haphazard habits, I did, in earlier years, tuck the flower beds in for winter—cutting back the dried stalks of perennials, composting the remains of annuals, tugging out the weeds I'd ignored all summer, installing a deep layer of mulch to keep everything safe from the cold. I have a shed full of rakes and spades and three-pronged cultivators because the neighborhood children used to descend in a pack to help me garden. One fall a bunch of them showed up in roller skates and didn't bother to change into shoes before they took up their tools.

Those children are grown now, like my own, and I don't tuck in my flower beds anymore. Year by year, the creatures who share this yard have been teaching me the value of an untidy garden. Monkey grass is invasive, in part because birds disperse its seeds by eating its berries, so Haywood continues to cut back the border, but it was hard not to be glad the hungry robins had something to eat on that cold day.

An unkempt garden offers more than just food for the birds. The late offspring of certain butterflies, like the black swallowtail, spend fall and winter sealed away in a chrysalis clinging to the dried stems in what's left of a summer garden. Others overwinter as eggs or caterpillars buried in the leaf litter beneath their host plants. Most species of native bees—or their fertilized queens, at least—hibernate underground during winter. An industrious gardener pulling up dead annuals could expose them to the cold, and one who mulches too thickly could block their escape in spring. Other beneficial insects like ladybugs, lacewings, and parasitic wasps spend winter in the hollow stems of old flowers.

These days we don't drag fallen limbs out to the street for the city chipper service to clean up, either. A good brush pile is a boon to ground-foraging birds, who eat insects from the decomposing wood, and to all manner of small animals hiding from predators or sheltering from the wind and snow.

Before I learned the worth of a messy yard, an alpha redbird once established his territory here. Flawless in his scarlet plumage, he was strong and loud and fearless, and he fiercely guarded the safflower feeder hanging just past our back deck. Cardinals will generally defer to bigger birds, or to birds who arrive at the feeder in flocks, but this redbird would not cede the airspace around that feeder for anyone.

I don't know how many years this yard was his territory—three, possibly four—but I have not seen another cardinal before or since who was quite so ferocious in defense of his own world. Though I can't say for certain it was always the same bird, it seemed so to me. And I believe it was the same bird I found one cold morning, when I walked outside after a nighttime snow, lying beneath the pear tree at the back of the yard.

Maybe it was just his time to go. But I think often of that stunning redbird lying crooked in the snow, a fallen battle flag, a bleeding wound, a Shakespearean hero come to a terrible end. And I can't help wondering if his fate might have been different if I had known back then to keep a dense brush pile in the yard for birds to shelter in on pitiless winter nights. Would he have survived to reign undisputed when the days finally warmed and it was time to sing again?

Praise Song for
the Praise Song of a
Song Sparrow in Winter

He came from somewhere north of here, and I did not expect him to stay. There has never been a song sparrow in this yard during our time here, but this one song sparrow has taken up residence. He sings from within the pine tree next to the driveway. He sings from the middle of the power line above the road. He sings from inside a holly bush at one end of the pollinator garden. All day long he sings and sings. It is a loud, piercing song that shudders his full body, a song that lifts straight through the clouds and far beyond the sky. All this long winter long, the song sparrow in his pine tree pulpit has been teaching me that one exuberant, unceasing song can change everything.

Hate to See That
Evening Sun Go Down

Winter ❧ Week 6

Feel your feet solid on the Earth. You have already arrived.

—THICH NHAT HANH, *How to Walk*

T o follow politics these days is to court bewilderment, denial,
complete despair. Too often I feel I am living in a country I no
longer recognize, a country determined to imperil every principle
I hold dear and many of the people I love, too. Immersing myself
in the natural world of my own backyard—or the nearby parks and
greenways, or the woods surrounding our friends' cabin on the
Cumberland Plateau—is the way I cope with whatever I think I
cannot bear.

I'm not trying to hide from the truth but to balance it, to remind
myself that there are other truths, too. I need to remember that the
earth, fragile as it is, remains heartbreakingly beautiful. I need to
give my attention to a realm that is indifferent to fretful human
mutterings and naked human anger, a world unaware of the hatred
and distrust taking over the news.

At heart, most people are good. This is one of my cardinal arti-
cles of faith, the principle upon which I have staked my entire

conscious life. Maybe that explains why, for far too long, I assumed that the foulest voices of the political din were rare and isolated, faint and fading. I was wrong about that. Like King Lear on the heath, I had "ta'en too little care" of those who are made vulnerable by what is happening in American politics.

It wasn't enough to write about the injustices. It wasn't enough to give money to people and organizations working full-time to combat evil in all its forms. For my own sake, I needed to find a way to pitch in directly.

It was not yet dawn when I left the house for my first tutoring shift at a Nashville public school that serves refugee families. I groaned when the alarm went off that freezing day at the end of January. But I felt better the second I walked into the school. Haywood is a teacher, and I was once a teacher, and I spent many hours in many schools as the mother of three children, but it has been some time since I felt the very specific kind of electricity that fills any place filled with teenagers. The flowing stream of humanity in the hallways—staff, teachers, the security guard, even the teenagers themselves—seemed more cheerful than I have ever felt at six forty-five in the morning.

Two hours later, after helping with a unit on the Harlem Renaissance, I was humming as I walked back to my car. I wasn't thinking about the cataclysmic state of my country. I was thinking about the bright, funny students I'd met in a class for English language learners. I was thinking about Bessie Smith singing "St. Louis Blues." But when I started my car, the radio came on, offering the usual news summary that opens each hour's programming. Two red lights later, my happiness was gone.

That's how my vow of resistance finally yielded to the appeal of retreat.

When I came to the third light, I turned left instead of continuing through it, and I drove to a little park in the woods where I often walk. There wasn't time before work to take the lake trail, my favorite path, but I walked as far as the dam and sat for a bit to watch a great blue heron fishing in the clear water. I listened to the invisible songbirds high in the treetops, and I watched the cold turtles climbing slowly onto fallen branches to warm themselves in the grace of a sunny day in January. For a few minutes, it was enough.

BURT'S SEED FOR QUALITY

A Seed in Darkest Winter

Winter ❧ Week 7

If I cultivate a flourishing, I want its reach to be wide.

—CAMILLE T. DUNGY, *Soil*

For most of my adult life, I wore a red coat when the weather got cold. It started when I was twenty-two and searching for new outerwear during what turned out to be my one winter in Philadelphia. I kept being drawn to a bright red peacoat in a mail-order catalog. Perhaps it reminded me of home in Alabama, the color of the ubiquitous cardinals perched among green pine needles, the color of camellia blossoms tucked among glossy leaves on branches that reached higher than our neighbors' windows.

My block in urban Philadelphia offered no such reminders of home. The birds outside my grad-school apartment were pigeons and house sparrows and starlings, gray or brown or black. Where were the blue jays singing their squeaky screen-door song, or the flickers with their merry red mustaches, or the red-breasted robins scratching for worms in the brown grass? Philadelphia lies within the year-round range of all three species, I knew, but no such birds ever found their way anywhere near my fourth-floor walkup on the four-lane surface road. I might as well have been looking for camellias.

From the moment it arrived, I adored that red peacoat. The Philly skies were steely and low, continually threatening snow or a bitter rain, and I felt happier swaddled in a cheerful bit of living color while the world turned itself into a nineteenth-century engraving all around me.

Even before I left Alabama, winter was my least-favorite season, a time when songbirds mostly cease their singing and small, furtive creatures find a secret place to sleep all day. Winter is the season of coats, the season of shoes. In summer I was a barefoot child in the emerald woods. In winter I sat indoors and watched it rain.

My mother's flower beds were always beautifully extravagant, even at ground-floor apartments we rented for no more than a year, and Mom coped with the wintertime blues by poring over gardening books and catalogs. I stuck with my red-coat cure. Then the zipper broke on my last red coat, and I couldn't find a replacement I liked. Turns out it didn't matter. Somewhere along the way I had stopped hating winter. I fell in love with the way the peeling bark and bare limbs of the sycamore reveal a ghost tree reaching for the sky, and the way the faded beech leaves cling to their branches and rustle in the wind like dry bells. A beech tree in a winter forest gives off its own light in the same way that dogwood blossoms in springtime look like tiny ground-borne suns.

I love the great horned owl's haunting courtship song and the crows' constant, multilayered conversation. There are good reasons not to make a habit of feeding wildlife—creatures who lose their fear of humans too often come to a bad end at the hands of fearful humans—but I do leave peanuts out for my wild neighbors before winter storms, when their survival may depend upon my help. I delight in watching the squirrels hiding their prizes under the leaf litter, and then watching the wily blue jays dig them up and carry them away to their own hidey-holes. I have come to welcome the gray, lowering skies because they mean I will have the trails at the park to myself.

Who could fail to embrace a season so beautiful and so fragile?

Even the most ideologically stubborn among us have finally come to understand how fragile winter truly is. It is only the first week of February, but the daffodils have already begun to bloom. There can be no reasonable argument about what is happening to the planet, now that daffodils so commonly bloom in February.

Nevertheless, the winter of old still returns from time to time, and the songbirds once again swarm my feeders. In the absence of insects, even the bluebirds will settle for sunflower hearts until I can get to the store for mealworms. When I leave for a walk on a night with temperatures in the teens, my eyes tear up, and the tears freeze to the inside of my glasses. The dog refuses to leave the driveway, plainly telling me that any creature with a warm shelter should not be walking in weather like this.

That's when I remember the garden catalogs, the pleasure of sitting under a blanket on a cold night and thumbing through page after page of flowers. One year a storm split one of our maple trees straight through the middle, and we had no choice but to take it down to a stump. When it was gone, there was a new sunny place in our yard, room for a whole new pollinator bed to feed our bees and butterflies. I picked out some promising varieties from an heirloom seed catalog, and then I looked them all up to make sure they were native to Middle Tennessee. By the time I'd come up with a plan for the new flower bed that included plants of varying heights and colors and blooming times, plants that are also compatible with the specific light and soil conditions of our yard and the specific needs of native insects, I felt as though I'd passed some kind of test.

I was so absorbed by the task of planning for spring that I completely forgot how long the wait for true springtime would be. I was thinking about the scent of turned earth, the feel of damp soil. I was feeling grateful that nature always renews itself, given even half a chance. I was remembering my favorite part of planting: the moment when the seedling, fragile as any lace-winged insect or hollow-boned nestling, somehow shoves the clods of earth aside and makes its way upward and outward. Searching for the light.

Praise Song for
the Dog's Marvelous Nose

Of all the canid noses, his is likely the weakest—weaker than a wolf's, weaker than a coyote's, weaker than a fox's—but still it is more marvelous than anything I can imagine. He puts his nose to the ground and sniffs. He puts his nose to the stop sign and sniffs. He puts his nose to the neighbor's garbage can and sniffs, sometimes rising up on his hind legs to get closer to a place that is higher than he can reach. In the spot where the neighborhood bobcat is known to cross the road, emerging from a hedge, he sniffs and sniffs. A neighbor tells me he saw a coyote early in the morning, standing across the street from his house, and that is the exact place where, later, my dog puts his nose. When we turn down a street where we rarely walk, for the sight lines there are poor and the traffic heavier than usual, the dog slows and finally stops. Has he caught the scent of the red fox that patrols this end of the neighborhood? I am only guessing, and no encouragement induces him to move along, much less to pick up speed. Something powerful holds him here, something that does not exist for me.

For him there is an entire world that exists beyond my ken, and in this matter he is not unique. For every living thing, there is a world that exists beyond my ken.

Done with Waiting

Winter ❧ Week 8

> I turned to see a crow standing in a low point in the creek,
> dipping its head in and whacking the surface hard with its
> wings, again and again, *whap whap, whap whap whap,*
> which I took to mean, of course, take your head out of
> your ass and be glad.
>
> —ROSS GAY, *The Book of Delights*

For more than a month, all we've had is rain. Until today, nothing but low skies and rain except for one early morning hour of something that might have been snow in the diamond air: white pellets winking past like falling stars, seen only in the periphery, invisible head-on. The cold that day brought the bluebirds to my heated birdbath for a drink.

The sky the bluebird carries on his back, as Thoreau observed, is nothing to the blue of this February sky. The golden kernels in my feeder are nothing to the light bouncing off the limbs of the oak tree reaching into the blue sky. I knew the day would be warm and bright before I opened my eyes.

The cardinals are the first to sing, and their song always heralds a pretty day in winter. *Birdy, birdy, birdy, birdy,* the male bird sings. *Birdy, birdy, birdy, birdy, cheer, cheer, cheer.* He seems to believe that

MARGARET RENKL

this warm day, coming as it does on the heels of a cold spell, is surely the beginning of spring, the season that is the point of all his singing: the season of courtship and mating, of nest building and nest guarding, of mate feeding and egg laying. The season of baby birds.

After an unseasonable time at home, my own babies are preparing to fly the nest come springtime. Our middle son graduated from college and commenced his job search just before the pandemic began. Phone interviews went well, on-site interviews were scheduled, and then everything shut down. It took four months for him to find a job during the hiring freezes of that time, and meanwhile his younger brother had come home, too, as his own college classes moved online. They couldn't believe it—so close to true freedom, and here they were again. "How is it possible that we're living in our childhood bedrooms?" they would say as the pandemic dragged on.

"I can't believe we're living in our childhood bedrooms," they were still saying a year later, even after the youngest had graduated, too, and even after vaccines had made life more livable again. They were both fully employed by then, but one had a job that required so much travel it made no sense to pay rent, and the other could not yet afford what landlords can charge in this growing city. Nearly two years after the pandemic began, they are finally looking for a place to share, hoping to be gone by spring.

I have loved having them here. Their older brother taught me that when they leave home this time, they will be leaving for good, so I am trying hard to be patient with winter this year, to settle into the season of waiting with more joy than I ever managed during winter's last gasp in the past.

But I have grown weary of walking on a silent trail, where the only sounds are my own footfall and the huff of my own breath on the uphill climb and the creak of bare branches in the wind. I am ready for the ringing bells of the spring peepers and the dawn chorus of the songbirds. I am ready for leaves to unfold on the branches and on the ground cover of the forest floor. I am ready for the moss to wake into a new green on the fallen trees, fallen so many years ago they no longer resemble trees. Unlike my sons, I am not ready to move past the past, but I am ready for something different, too, something new and urgent and thrumming with blood and sap and life. I am learning that it is possible to want two contrary things at once. I want nothing to change. I want everything to change.

A day like today is a reminder that in most ways, dangerous ways, spring is already here, heaving in on blue skies and puffy clouds and sunshine, long before its time. It's impossible not to worry. It's also impossible not to glory in the glorious day. "Birdy, birdy, birdy, birdy," sings the redbird. "Birdy, birdy, birdy, birdy, cheer, cheer, cheer." My heart sings, too. I can't help myself. Beauty and light will always be their own reward.

5.58

1.89

7.54

7.81

7.44

4.63

3.07

7.65

3.47

Fig.1.

Protractor, Rule and Square. Designed by Walter W. Hart, University of Wisconsin.
Printed for C. Smith and Company.

It's a Mystery

Winter ❧ *Week 9*

High winds and heavy rains always cause provisional things to tumble out of our trees—small branches and birds' nests, but also errant Frisbees and Nerf darts lost years before. When the rains finally let up one day, I wasn't surprised to see an unfamiliar object on the deck outside my back door. By the time I found it, though, it was soaked through, and in the near-dark I couldn't quite make out what it was. I've seen screech owls and barred owls and great horned owls in this yard—could it be an owl pellet? Owls cough up the undigestible remains of their meals in a tidy rounded package, but I had never seen one in real life before.

At slightly longer than three inches it was awfully big for an owl pellet, though great horned owls have been known to regurgitate pellets that large. Its shape and color and its position on the back deck, just below a maple tree where I have often seen an owl perched for hunting, certainly pointed to that possibility. But there were no bones in the outside layer, no teeth or beaks or claws poking up. Even on the outside, owl pellets almost always display some evidence of a meal.

When the image-search feature on my phone could neither confirm nor rule out the ID, I did what I always do when I'm confused: I posted the picture to social media and asked for help from the naturalists online. They, too, thought it was likely too big to be an owl pellet. They, too, observed the lack of undigested body parts. And they noticed some other problems: "The longer hairs don't seem to be from their usual prey," wrote one naturalist.

"The fur looks like deer," noted another. "If you spot an owl taking out a deer, please record video."

Naturalists can be real wags.

The discussion shifted to the possibility that this object had emerged from another kind of creature altogether—and from the other end of the creature, as well. "For me," wrote yet another naturalist, "the lack of visible bones, the 'looseness' of the structure, especially with all the free hairs (though soaking rain might cause a pellet to soften and start to come apart), and what appear to be quite a few conifer needles (suggesting this animal was eating from the ground) have me leaning towards mammal scat. None of these rule out pellet definitively though. The rounded shape does seem more like a pellet than a carnivore scat."

The carnivore most likely to produce waste of this particular shape, size, and color is a coyote. Behind our house there's a small patch of woods, three or four acres between the houses at the end of our street and the houses on a parallel street. Three different neighbors have lost dogs to the coyotes in those woods over the years. But the number of free-roaming cats around here has always made me think that coyotes don't live in our neighborhood so much as pass through it on occasion. Whenever Haywood can't sleep, he sits on our front stoop in the dark and looks at the stars. Several times he has seen a pair of coyotes trot past our house. One of them is always a few yards behind the other, but they are clearly a team, moving in a purposeful way from one end of the street to the other. Sometimes the lead coyote will glance in Haywood's direction without breaking stride, but neither of them ever stops. Surely one of those secretive creatures would not be bold enough to relieve itself on our deck?

Out of nothing more than hope, I did a little more clicking around online and brought myself back to believing I had an owl pellet on my hands, and a really large one at that. "I think I'll bring it inside and let it dry out for a few days and then cut into it," I told the naturalists.

With a promise to post pictures documenting the dissection, I grabbed some kitchen tongs and went back outside to lift my prize onto a saucer. As soon as I picked it up, I knew it was too light to be any kind of dung. There was no doubt now—I'd found my first owl pellet!

I brought it inside and showed it to Haywood. "Something wonderful fell out of the tree next to the deck," I said. "Guess what it is."

He peered at the drenched object I was holding out on a teacup saucer. A wary look crossed his face. He appeared to be choosing his words carefully: "What do *you* think it is?"

"I'm not absolutely sure, but I think it's an owl pellet, most likely from a great horned owl. It's awfully large for a pellet, even from an owl that big, but I've been looking at pictures online, and it's definitely . . ."

My husband was visibly struggling for composure.

I stopped. "What?"

"Remember this morning, when you thought the vacuum cleaner was busted? Turns out there was just a wad of stuff plugging up the hose."

Oh.

Not deer fur: dog hair. Not evidence of a ground forager: Christmas-tree needles.

I couldn't decide which was worse, disappointment or embarrassment. Over on social media, the wags were amused. "A Hoover pellet," wrote one.

"A Hoover hooter pellet," added another.

Praise Song for
Mole Hands in Coyote Scat

It's their hands that kill me every time. How hopefully I check the trail camera for a glimpse of the dear, nearsighted opossum resting her small pink fingers on the water dish I set out on a stump during droughts, the dainty way she holds the rim of the dish while she leans forward to drink. How careful I am not to let the dog outside when the squirrel, her nipples puffed from nursing, sits up on her hind legs and holds her thumbless hands close to her chest when she sees me at the back door. How still the deer mouse in the toolshed holds her own hands, for only the barest instant, when I open the door to flood the room with light. The deer mouse is the wild neighbor I see most fleetingly of all the fleet creatures who share our yard.

But I love the mole hands best of all. I delight in their absurd fleshy pinkness, six-fingered but so human, as though a child putting together a kit had attached the wrong parts to the mole's velvet body. I love those hands, though I've only ever seen a mole in photos or in death, poisoned by a neighbor and crawled to the surface to die. Perhaps that heartbreak is why the photo I saw of little pink mole hands poking out of coyote scat didn't break my heart.

Somebody was hungry. Somebody fed the hungry one.

The Crow Family

Winter ✤ *Week 10*

Glossy and rowdy / and indistinguishable. / The deep
muscle of the world.

—MARY OLIVER, "Crows"

Even in late February, many of the most interesting creatures
are still asleep. The cheery chipmunks are bundled into their
tunnels beneath my house. The queen bumblebees are curled into
their chambers in the soil. Somewhere nearby, the resident rat
snake is also underground, and at the park the snapping turtles and
bullfrogs are tucked into the mud at the bottom of the lake. The
overwintering butterfly chrysalids are sleeping in the garden, and
the monarch butterflies are sleeping in their Mexican wintering
grounds. Everything is waiting for the world to wake. My flower
beds are nothing but a jumble of dried stems and matted clumps,
a collection of dead vegetation. Even remembering the purpose
behind this untidiness, I take no comfort from my garden in
February.

I miss the singing most of all. During winter we do have songbirds in Middle Tennessee, some of them yearlong residents and
some of them visitors passing time in this warmer climate until

they can return to their nesting grounds up north. The fussy chickadees will call out to defend their claim on the bird feeders. And the Carolina wrens who sometimes nest in the hanging pots under our eaves will stand on a fence post and chirrup their irritation into the gray sky. But none of this is singing. It's not the same as waking into a morning full of birdsong.

And yet.

Winter can be the best time of year for backyard bird-watching. The mockingbirds are finally interested in the suet balls they disdained all summer, and the gorgeous blue jays, their bright colors even bluer against the sepia backdrop of winter, carry away the unshelled nuts I set along the deck railing. The dark-eyed juncos who spent all summer in the far north are here now, hopping around in the leaf litter, picking up the safflower seeds the tufted titmice push out of the feeder in their search for the sunflower seeds they prefer.

Now the downy woodpeckers, with their striped wings, come and go from the peanut feeder, not nearly so cautious in my presence as in the days of summertime plenty. They swoop to their feast with the characteristic undulating flight of their kind. In the years when I get around to hanging Christmas garland, I always try to arrange it in a way that mimics the arc of their flight.

On especially cold mornings, every songbird in Middle Tennessee, it seems, comes to my back deck to enjoy the heated birdbath. There can be six or eight bluebirds gathered in a ring around the edge of it, dipping their beaks into the bowl over and over again while the air above the warm water puffs into fog in the cold.

In winter the red-tailed hawk sits unmoving in the bare branches of trees, a perch where she is invisible to me at any other time of year. Now I can see even the claws on her great yellow feet extending beyond the fluffed feathers she has drawn around them. The crows know very well that she is there, and they have a few furious words for her as she waits, calmly surveying them as they swoop around her head, close but not too close.

Of all the backyard birds, the corvids—the crows and the blue jays—are most familiar to me. They don't nest in plain view as the bluebirds do, or stand on the fence posts and sing like the mockingbirds. They don't conduct daring aerial exploits before my very eyes, close enough to touch, as the hummingbirds do in summer. I love the crows not because they are exotic but because they are kindred creatures. I see in them my own kind.

Corvids are uncannily like us in unexpected ways. Ravens have been known to windsurf at the beach, holding a bit of driftwood in their feet for ballast. Crows will ride down snowy roofs on flat objects they put to use as sleds. Again and again, they haul their toy to the roofline and toboggan down the slope in what looks for all the world like playing.

After they quarrel, crows take care to make up with one another, but they can recognize human faces and will hold a grudge against someone who frightens them or causes them harm. They can even teach their children to maintain the grudge, the corvid equivalent of the Hatfields and McCoys. When a crow dies, other crows gather around its body. To mourn? To bid their friend farewell? We don't know, but they are our nearest avian kin, living together in families, creating tools, and solving problems—even, in a way, making art out of found objects. They stalk along the ground as though they own the place, like certain people I know.

Despite their legendary intelligence, I have the same issues with corvids that I have with raptors. I love them, but love is sometimes a struggle, especially during the breeding season, when they poach the young from songbird nests to feed to their own young.

During migration seasons, crows will devour the exhausted song-birds themselves. Nothing is harder to love about the natural world—or the human world—than its ceaseless brutality.

But in winter, crows become my favorites again. They are perfectly designed for this season, black against a gray sky, a three-dimensional silhouette. Unlike other birds, who grow quiet in winter, crows continue to speak to one another even on the coldest days. American crows remain together as a family through the seasons, with parents and young from several nesting years working together to find food and fend off predators. I watch them grooming one another in the high branches: one crow will nibble at another crow's head or neck, and the other crow will tilt its face this way and that, presenting the itchy places for attention, one by one. I remember the way my mother, when I crawled into the big bed between her and Dad, would run her fingers lightly down my arm, the way Dad would scratch my back. I think of the way I wiggled, the way I, too, twisted this way and that, to make sure they reached every inch of skin.

Crow families always recall to me my grandparents, who lost their home to fire when their family was very young and had to move into my great-grandparents' house just down the road. There must have been a time when my grandparents considered moving back out, but they never did. Maybe they came to understand the practicality of a multigenerational household, the way there was always someone home to help with the children or, later, after my great-grandparents grew frail, with the older generation. Maybe they simply couldn't imagine living apart by then. Maybe they just loved living together, all three generations in the same small house.

Those days are gone. Even during the pandemic, when the multigenerational household became more common than it had been for generations, my sons seemed to feel something almost like shame about coming home, as though home were by definition a place a child grows up to escape. How do you meet a life partner, or even just a date, if you have to admit you live with your parents?

This situation does not recall to them the stories they have heard of my grandparents, of my mother and my uncle, of Papa Doc and Mama Alice, gathered on the porch of a mild winter evening, while light streaked the sky and oak limbs creaked in the wind. How they sat together and talked. Or maybe just listened.

I am trying to listen.

Sometimes the neighborhood crows sit in the branches and call out, one to another, a talk that continues even as they fly toward their roost in the last light of these short days. The crow's *Caw!* is recognizable to the human ear, but the birds actually have more than twenty different calls, not even counting the "subsong" sounds they make: clacking and cooing and rattling and clicking. I don't know what the crows are saying to the other crows, but I like to listen in. It's a gift to watch them living their intricate lives so visibly while the trees are bare. This is their world, but I have no trouble understanding what they are saying to the red-tailed hawk: *Away! Go away!* It may be their message for me as well.

The Knothole

Plant life, like all life, is the subject of constant revision.

—ANN PATCHETT, *This Is the Story of a Happy Marriage*

The time for planting trees is fall. Planting after the heat of summer gives a young tree the chance to settle into its new surroundings before going dormant for winter, and fall rains help it to establish deeper roots that give it resilience when the blistering heat of summer returns. Things can still go wrong, of course—it's hard not to worry about a tender sapling, bare and cold in winter—but a dormant tree, even a very young one, is mostly safe from hard freezes.

The problem is that these once-predictable patterns keep getting upended. It can be ninety degrees one winter day and drop below freezing that very night. The gentle rains of fall have become the torrential floods of winter. Paying attention to what is happening to the natural world can be a form of self-torment, and I sometimes wonder how much longer I can keep seeing the losses that surround me and not descend into a kind of despair that might as well be called madness. Some days I'm one headline away from becoming Lear, raging into the storm.

For thirty years I built my life: childhood, school, profession, marriage, the birth of my first child. Exactly thirty years. For Haywood and me, the time of caretaking, of providing for our children and for our aging parents, also lasted exactly thirty years. And now I have entered the last third of my life, if what we mean by *last third* is whatever happens after everything you were working toward has already happened.

My grandmother and great-grandmother each lived well into their nineties, as did both of Haywood's grandmothers. Even my father-in-law, whom we lost only last year, survived to be almost ninety-three despite congestive heart failure and a pandemic that hit the elderly especially hard. I don't expect to have thirty years left myself—I have lived long enough to see how unreliable good health can be, how easily it can be snatched away—but I persist in thinking that I have entered the last third of my life. I just put the emphasis on *last* and not on *third*.

I still have work that matters to me. I still have faraway places to see, a life to share with Haywood, perhaps grandchildren someday. All endings are also beginnings. This is what I tell myself again and again.

On a late winter day when the relentless rains let up for a bit, I drove to the park an hour before sunset to walk on the muddy trails. The woods were as lovely as they ever are after a rain: the creeks full of rushing water, the gray bark of the fallen trees slick with moss. Above the trail, the limbs of the living trees creaked in the rising wind, the kind of sound that makes your heart ache for reasons too far beyond words to explain. Too early, the forest understory was already greening up, but the eastern towhees scratching for insects in what was left of the fall leaves were not in any way sorry about the too-early arrival of spring.

As darkness began to gather in earnest, I turned to head back the way I'd come. A few hundred yards on, my eyes caught on a tree I hadn't noticed when I was walking in the other direction. About seven feet up the trunk was a knothole, a place where a limb long ago broke off and let water in to rot the wood. Perhaps a woodpecker helped to deepen it, too, and gave the water more purchase over time. The hole was a grotto in the thickly grooved bark of the stalwart oak, a hiding place that reached far into the mass of that old tree. Who knows how many woodland creatures had crept into that crevice over the years to nest, to shelter from the wind and rain, to hide from predators, or to wait for prey?

But a creature lurking inside was not what singled this knothole out among the hundreds, even thousands, I passed in the park that day. What caught my eye was a cluster of chickweed seedlings colored the new green of springtime, so bright they seemed to glow. They were growing in the loam inside the knothole. Far above the ground, a hole made by decay in a living tree had become a cold frame, a natural greenhouse that let in light and kept out frost. Life in death in life.

On the way home I thought about that mundane miracle, that commonplace resurrection. Even now, with the natural world in so much trouble—even now, with the patterns of my daily life changing in ways I don't always welcome or understand—radiant things are bursting forth in the darkest places, in the smallest nooks and deepest cracks of the hidden world. I mean to keep looking every single day until I find them.

Wild Joy

Winter ❧ Week 12

Notes on springtime and on anything else that comes to mind of an intoxicating nature.

—E. B. WHITE, *One Man's Meat*

March comes in like a lion, except when it comes in like a lamb. Or when it comes in like a chorus, a symphony, and an exquisitely choreographed ballet all at once, a performance so breathtaking it could not possibly be replicated. It is replicated anyway, one day after another.

Cue the waking insects stirring in the leaf litter. Cue the flashing bluebirds swooping from the bare maple branches to reap the insects stirring in the leaf litter. Cue the fox in his magnificent coat shining in the moonlight, his ears pricked, his tail curled around his beautiful fox feet. Cue the hard brown buds, waiting, waiting, all through winter but just beginning to quiver. Any day now—*any day!*—they will warm into blossom.

I treasure every iridescent green bee waking to feed on the first vanishing bloodroot flower, the first ephemeral spring beauty, the first woodland violet and cutleaf toothwort. Soon there will be trilliums and trout lilies, too. Any day now, toadshade trilliums and trout lilies!

If you tell me I don't deserve this joy, you are telling me nothing I don't already know. From the very first hominid to rise up on bare feet and stumble across a field of blooming grass, we have been burning this world down. I know that. I am in love with the mild light of the coming springtime anyway, with the shivering joy of the coming springtime, with all the beguiling creatures of the coming springtime.

Come to the woods and stand with me in the sunshine beneath the trees. Watch the bluebirds diving for insects. Watch them peeking into the nest holes the woodpeckers carved out years ago. Listen to the cry of the woodpeckers in the echoing woods. Let it lift your heart. Let it still your busy hands and feet, and let it still your worried mind. Listen with everything you are. With all you are, listen for the hum and flutter of the waking world. The upland chorus frogs are singing. It is a song of full-throated promise.

It's beginning again. It's all beginning again.

It's true that most of what is greening up in these woods right now isn't native to the American South. March is a stark reminder of how thoroughly plants imported from Europe and Asia have escaped their gardens and taken over the surrounding fields and forests. Sap is rising in the canes of Japanese honeysuckle, and sap is rising in the branches of Bradford pear trees. While our native maples and oaks are still sleeping, and the poison ivy that coils around them, too, the invasive vinca vines in the understory are waking up into greenness. I can hardly help greeting them with joy.

I refuse to quell this joy. It's possible to understand what invasive species are doing to the woods and still feel the leaping heart of joy in the presence of greenness. It's entirely possible to exult in birdsong and miniature flowers peeking out from the dead leaves of autumn. In this troubled world, it would be a crime to snuff out any flicker of happiness that somehow flames up into life.

We are creatures built for joy. At the very saddest funerals, we can hear a funny story about our lost beloved, and, God help us, we laugh. We can stagger out of an appointment where a person in a white coat has given us the news we think we cannot bear to hear, and still we smile at the baby in the checkout line clapping her chubby hands at the balloons by the cash register or kicking her feet in pleasure at the sight of a stranger's smile.

This is who we are. The very best of who we are.

The world is burning, and there is no time to put down the water buckets. For just an hour, put down the water buckets anyway. Take your cue from the bluebirds, who have no faith in the future but who build the future nevertheless, leaf by leaf and straw by straw, shaping them into the roundness of the world.

Turn your face up to the sky. Listen. The world is trembling into possibility. The world is reminding us that this is what the world does best. New life. Rebirth. The greenness that rises out of ashes.

Ephemeral

Winter ❧ Week 13

It's almost impossible to think about nature without thinking about time.

—Verlyn Klinkenborg, *The Rural Life*

The cabin is perched right on a bluff in the woods of the Cumberland Plateau. Built from trees harvested a hundred years earlier on our friends' family land, it is my favorite place on Earth. Our friends urge Haywood and me to use it whenever they can't get there on a weekend themselves. Endangered plants and animals live in the shelter of Lost Cove, which opens below the bluff: Morefield's leather flower and Cumberland rosinweed, the eastern small-footed bat and the Allegheny woodrat. The painted snake-coiled forest snail is so rare it lives only in Franklin County, Tennessee. The cabin is a place of quiet and stillness. A retreat from the world. Every time we visit, we think about how calm our lives would be if we lived in a peaceful place like this all year long.

When we arrive on this weekend in mid-March, we see that the hidden basin in the woods behind the cabin—less a basin than a depression between folds of ancient land, imperceptible in summer and fall—has begun to fill up again. This pool of black water is my favorite thing about my favorite place in the high woods of the Cumberland Plateau. The ephemeral pond is coming back.

The soil on this bluff has been gathering for millennia, but in most places it is so thin you marvel that any tree, much less these many and massive trees, could grow here. But in the low place that is beginning to be a pond, the soil is thick and rich, teeming with invisible life. It has been holding on to leaves for as long as there have been trees in this forest. It has been holding on to everything—leaves but also acorns, fallen branches, a long-dead tree balanced above the water on one long-dead limb.

For much of the year the pond, dried up and completely concealed beneath last fall's leaves, doesn't exist. The only sign of it is the place on the forest floor where the leaves remain inexplicably damp. Other leaves dry out and blow about with every thermal that rises from below the bluff, but these leaves stay wet. In fall they grow darker and damper still.

One bright winter day, following a big rain or a heavy, melting snow, you realize the leaves in the half-acre shallow are suddenly giving back the blue sky and the sentinels of bare trees towering above them. From the nearby path it looks as though someone has buried a large mirror in the sleeping woods and carelessly tried to hide it with old leaves.

Then you notice that the mirror is growing.

In winter this pond can't rightly be called a pond, but the rains keep coming. Fog gathers and condenses. Water drips from every cloud-drenched tree. The pond remains muddy at the margins, clotted with any wafting thing the winds can bring, but the water spreads out and deepens. Human beings have had no hand in making this pond; you can tell because it is not bounded by banks or populated by fish.

Emerging from the layers of windfall, the water is black, as black as volcanic glass, because the soil below it is richer and blacker than any soil I have ever seen. I know this from knowing the pond in dry seasons. I don't need to prove it to myself again now. I don't kick the leaves aside to inspect it. I don't so much as nudge it with my toe. This soil is precious. It must not be disturbed.

In time the pond will engulf the soil, spreading far beyond the margins of the gathering mud. As it spreads, it will become home to a vast number of wetland plants and small creatures that have spent all fall and winter buried in the soil of the ghost pond. Dormant crustacean eggs, the larvae of aquatic insects, sleeping salamanders—all will be brought to waking life again by the rain.

And then an entire array of beautiful creatures will find one another and lay their eggs. This pond that is too transitory to support fish is the perfect nursery for amphibians whose eggs too often become someone else's food in other ponds and creeks. Spotted salamanders live underground, but soon they will climb to the surface to mate and lay eggs in this pool. When they get here, they may find that the marbled salamanders have arrived first. The mole salamanders will stay in the shallowest spots on the edges of the pond. They can live nowhere else on this mountain.

As the pond fills, the wood frogs and the pickerel frogs will arrive, and the spring peepers. Their mating songs will turn the spring nights into symphonies. The toads, too, will come to lay their eggs. The pond that is not a pond will become an incubator for every salamander larva and tadpole on this bluff.

They must be quick in their waking, though, for the sharp-eyed crows have been waiting for them. Our friends have seen the birds standing in the mud in a great black circle, scooping up toads and tree frogs as soon as they emerge from the water. Nor are crows the only danger: winter-sleeping predators are waking, too. Can you see the garter snake beneath the raised branch of the dead tree at the edge of the water? I can't. The frogs, intent on finding one another, cannot see it, either. It is not meant to be seen.

In summer they will all be gone. The pond, vanished into the shimmering heat, will be hidden once more beneath brush and leaves.

Praise Song for
a Spring I Was Not
Alive to See

On the first day of spring, I won't think of flowers or greening leaves. I will think of something I have never actually seen: my grandmother as a young teacher. She is walking to school—a straight shot down a red dirt road and then a turn that takes her through the graveyard next to the church. My mother and my uncle, younger than I can hardly picture to myself, are running ahead, laughing, but the little dog is beside my grandmother, walking. The sky is blue, for of course the sky is blue. More birds than I have ever heard, even in springtime, sing from the fields and from the tree line that sections the land into fields. The sun is shining on my grandmother's hair, browner than it ever was during the many years we lived together on the same Earth. The sun shines, too, on the stack of books she carries in her arms, and on the golden fur of the dog who will spend all day under her desk, waiting to walk her home again.

So many birds are singing and singing and singing.

The Season of Waking

Spring ❧ Week 1

The world does not proceed according to our plans. The world is an old dog, following us around the kitchen with its eyes. The world understands us. We understand nothing, control less.

Today it is springtime. Every green thing has grown greener as the pines send out new growth. Every brown thing is taking on green as the hardwoods wake into warmth. But tonight the black sky is spitting out ice, and the green sap rising will likewise turn to ice in the dark. Some of these frail green things will be blasted forever, but most will live. Life is what life does.

We, too, will live. In the morning we will wake and rejoice, for we are once more among the living.

Who Will Mourn Them When
They Are Gone?

Spring ❧ Week 2

You can't come back to something that is gone.

—RICHARD POWERS, *The Overstory*

On this gray day when the only shred of color is the muted green of the hemlocks and white pines, still more gray than green, I am thinking of the eastern hardwood forests, the forests dense with oaks—more species of oak than I can name—and dense, as well, with sweet gum and birch and poplar and hemlock and hickory and pine. And of course I think of the majestic, doomed American chestnut, once four billion strong. It was so dominant and so widespread, legend has it, that a squirrel in Maine could make its way to Georgia, leaping from chestnut to chestnut, without ever once touching the ground. Now all but entirely gone. Those trees, so thick and so plentiful with life-sustaining nuts— and not just for hungry squirrels and hungry bears but for hungry humans, too—might have survived our axes, but they could not survive the blight that hitched a ride on our ships.

I try to imagine the primeval chestnut forest and the creatures who made it their home, the timber wolves and panthers driven from our lands as the forests fell, creatures kept away now by our controlling fears. I think of the birds who once roosted in those branches and who no longer live here, or anywhere, and I think of the insects whose churring wings no longer fill my summers, the grasshoppers and the lightning bugs, and I think of the toads hunting moths beneath the lampposts and the bats hunting moths in the damp night skies.

All gone now. I have not seen a turtle or a toad in our yard for two decades or more, and only a single grasshopper each of the last two years. The bats and the lightning bugs are visibly diminishing, fewer and fewer with every passing summer. The flock of cedar waxwings that comes in winter to our hollies has grown so small I wonder if *flock* is still the right word for them.

This is one of the things that tugs hard against the possibility of retiring to a quieter, slower place. If we sell our house, the next owner will tear it down, along with all its trees and all its flowers and all its berry-bearing vines and shrubs, and then where will the bluebirds go? Where will the butterflies feed and the lightning bugs sleep? What high grass will the shy rat snake slip through? After we are dead it will all happen anyway, Haywood reminds me, through no choice we make ourselves.

Suddenly, it seems, time is something I think about all the time. We don't know how many days we will be given, but we all know those days will give out sooner than we like to ponder. Now I ponder it endlessly. Last year, almost overnight, my father-in-law went from mostly fine to clearly failing. Pneumonia took him in days, just as our youngest child was finishing his degree. In the space of two weeks, barely more than a breath, the world turned for Haywood and me: all our children grown, all our parents gone.

The future no longer spreads out before me like an endless opportunity, like a sensible vessel for any plans I might conceive. It doesn't seem fair that the future is contracting exactly as each day has begun to pass so quickly I can hardly remember one from another.

I am thinking about time in both directions now—not just a future that will roll on without me, and without so many of the creatures I love, but a past I was not alive to remember. I think about the American chestnuts, today so rare that their locations are often closely kept secrets among researchers trying to understand why this scant handful survived. All the vanishing plants and creatures I love so dearly are, I know, only the barest remnant of the abundance this landscape once sustained. There were twice as many songbirds the year I was born as there are now, and even that teeming number is paltry by comparison to those who lived when chestnuts reigned over the eastern forests.

One of my college professors told our class a story—I don't remember to what pedagogical end—about his first spring in Alabama, during the cacophonous songbird courtship season. The birds outside his home study were so loud, he said, that he could not think straight, but it was already so hot that he could not close the windows. And thereby did this new-minted professor, arriving in rural Alabama from the cool of Michigan, discover the need for air-conditioning.

I have no idea why I remember this story, which my teacher told only in passing, when I have forgotten so many other things about that class, including the subject of the course itself. Perhaps I heard it the same semester I took my first environmental biology course and was beginning to understand how fragile the natural world really is, the world that had always felt like my sturdiest home.

Nearly forty years have passed since I was in college, and I find myself thinking of the undergraduates who plod through the landscape that welcomed me at their age, a landscape so altered as to bewilder me when I visit. In years to come, will they remember with nostalgia what must seem even now like a magnificent chorus of birdsong pouring down from the trees? Are we all, generation upon generation, destined to mourn what seems in this moment impossibly abundant but is already far on its way to being gone?

The world will always be beautiful to those who look for beauty. Throats will always catch when the fleeing clouds part fleetingly and the golden moon flashes into existence and then winks out again. Tears will always spring up at the wood thrush singing through the echoing trees, at the wild geese crying as they fly. A soul touched by the scent of turned soil or sun-warmed grass, a spirit moved by crickets singing in the grass, will spend a lifetime surrounded by wonder even as songbirds drop one by one from the poisoned sky and crickets fall silent in the poisoned grass.

Apocalyptic stories always get the apocalypse wrong. The tragedy is not the failed world's barren ugliness. The tragedy is its clinging beauty even as it fails. Until the very last cricket falls silent, the beauty-besotted will find a reason to love the world.

Praise Song for
the Maple Tree's First Green

"Nature's first green is gold," Robert Frost wrote, "her hardest hue to hold." Even as a schoolgirl, I understood the paradox of those lines—of green beginning in gold, of leaf beginning in flower—but I had never seen that paradox for myself. I thought it must be a New England phenomenon not replicated in the piney woods of Alabama. An Alabama girl who is drunk on poetry makes allowances like that. I'd never seen the woods fill up with snow, either.

But every year the sugar maples in my Tennessee yard flower in pale catkins, clusters of miniature flowers descending from long filaments. Every year I walk down my street and stand where I can regard the trees in full. From a distance, it's a miser's hoard. It's Rapunzel in her tower. It's a sun, a thousand suns, come to Earth. I stare and stare, trying to commit it to memory, for tomorrow the flowers will be shrouded by leaves. Because Frost was right: nothing gold can stay.

LIST

PLATE

CIII. Mountain Fringe, . .
CIV. Fireweed, ...
CV. Steeple Bush, . . .
CVI. *Pink Knotweed, . .
CVII. Purple Loosestrife, .
CVIII. Meadow-beauty, . .
CIX. *Large Sea Pink, . .
CX. Rose Mallow, . . .
CXI. *Musk Mallow, . . .
CXII. Marsh St. John's-
wort, ...
CXIII. Tick Trefoil, . . .
CXIV. Bouncing Bet, . . .
CXV. Purple Gerardia, . .
CXVI. Joe-Pye-weed, . . .
CXVII. *Wild Columbine, . .
CXVIII. Wake Robin, . . .
CXIX. *Painted Cup, . . .
CXX. *Pitcher Plant,
CXXI. Wood Lily, ...
CXXII. Turk's Cap Lily,
CXXIII. Butterfly-weed, .
CXXIV. Trumpet Honeysuckle,
CXXV. *Cardinal Flower,
CXXVI. Liverwort, . . .
CXXVII. *Bird-foot Violet,
CXXVIII. Dog Violet,

CXXIX. Bluets, . . .
CXXX. Wild Geranium,
CXXXI. Skull-cap, . . .
CXXXII. *Common Speedwell,
CXXXIII. Wild Lupine, .
CXXXIV. *Purple Fringed
Iris, . .
CXXXV. Self-heal, . . .
CXXXVI. *Arethusa, . . .
CXXXVII. Blue Vetch, .
CXXVIII. *Peppermint,
CXXXIX. Blueweed, . . .
CXL. *Pickerel-weed,
CXLI. *Harebell,

The Names of Flowers

Spring ❧ Week 3

Their names alone serve as a clew to their entire
histories, giving us that sense of companionship with
our surroundings which is so necessary to the full
enjoyment of outdoor life.

—Mrs. William Starr Dana,
How to Know the Wild Flowers

Stickywilly plants are nearly universal across the temperate
world, but their blossoms are so slight and so transitory that
you may believe you've never seen one. And perhaps you haven't—
they are easy to miss, even in weedy places, even if you happen to
be wandering there while the spring ephemerals are blooming
beneath the bare trees. April brings the stickywilly's four-petaled,
starlike flowers, but they are so small and close to green, even in
full bloom, that I must stoop and peer to tell whether I am looking
at buds or blossoms. Sometimes I only know I've been among
them because their seeds have come into the house with me, clinging to my socks.

Naturalists call the plant by its botanical name, *Galium aparine*.
It grows nearly everywhere and offers itself for many human uses:
as a hot drink, in a cake, as a salve for eczema, or as protection from

scurvy. But it goes by so many common names that stickywilly recipes passed down in rural families are hard to share because it would not be clear to others what wildflower, when dried and brewed, actually serves as a half-decent substitute for coffee. Is it catchweed? Bobby button or bedstraw or cleaverwort? Possibly it's cleavers, or clivers, or any of the nearly endless riffs on the plant's tendency to cling: stickyweed, stickybob, stickybud, stickyback, sticky molly, sticky grass, stickyjack, stickeljack, gripgrass, whippy-sticks. Shall I keep going? I could keep going for days.

I think of the serviceberry trees that bloom soon after the stickywillies. The simple serviceberry is native to every state except Hawaii. In the old days, the serviceberry's five-petaled blossoms heralded springtime, blooming just as snow melted on winding roads, just as mountain passes cleared. People who had spent all winter in isolation saw the serviceberry in bloom and knew that circuit-riding preachers would be along soon to perform the weddings and funeral services that snow had long delayed.

As with the stickywilly and all beloved wild plants, this harbinger of spring has many common names. What we call a serviceberry here in Tennessee is what people in other regions call shadbush, sarvis, juneberry, saskatoon, sugarplum, and chuckley pear. By whatever name they are locally called, the flowers were a welcome sight for the generations who came before us. Winter was over at last. Bright new life could begin.

Serviceberries are not much of a welcome sight anymore. So thoroughly have they been displaced from our cultivated landscapes that most Americans are unlikely to recognize this very American tree. For us, springtime means flowers that evolved for ecosystems in Europe and Asia. Those cheerful tulips and daffodils came here from northern Europe. The ubiquitous golden sprays of forsythia, the star magnolia, the flowering quince, the

Yoshino cherry, the Bradford pear—all came to us from Asia, where the growing season so closely matches the heat and humidity of the American South.

But I embrace the old-timey plants that evolved to feed wildlife, the plants with names that change from place to place and people to people. And I will always insist on the homely names of my Wiregrass ancestors. It was stickywilly in the fields of Lower Alabama, and it remains stickywilly to me all these years later in Tennessee. What you call the wildflowers will tell you who you are.

The Beautiful World beside
the Broken One

Spring ❧ Week 4

When does otherness dissolve?

—LILY HOANG, *A Bestiary*

A three-week bout with Covid turned me into a person I didn't recognize—a hopeless, coughing, exhausted person. I lay in bed, phone in hand, skipping from news site to news site: refreshing, clicking, scrolling, scrolling, scrolling. The news was always bad, every update worse than the one before. I began to think the fever in my body had somehow leached into the world, burning it into unrecognizability just outside my bedroom walls.

But there's another world that has always existed apart from and alongside civilization. While I was sick it had changed, too, in the age-old turning of the earth. By the time I could walk outside again, springtime had come to Tennessee.

The invasive but lovely deadnettle had turned the ditch next to our house into a cascading drift of purple. Every year it reminds me of Alice Walker's words: "I think it pisses God off if you walk by the color purple in a field somewhere and don't notice it." In the woods beside the cabin on the Cumberland Plateau, trout lilies were opening near toadshade and bloodroot and mayapple, all of them reaching up from the cold soil to bloom in the brief sunlight of early spring, before the trees leaf out and the forest overstory draws in all the available light.

This time of year, tree limbs are still mostly bare, but the songbirds have registered the mild light, and their courtship season has begun. The television may be full of terror, and the terror may be growing with every passing hour, but the trees are full of music. The blue jays sing their tender whisper song, and the quarrelsome beeping of the Carolina chickadee is transformed into a ringing four-note song of love: *fee-bee-fee-bay, fee-bee-fee-bay.* The redbird, too, serenades a female, and if you follow the song to its source, you might see him bringing his mate a seed or a grub, demonstrating his fitness as her partner. In the avian world, a grub is an engagement ring.

Alas for the poor grubs, and alas for the earthworms struggling to the surface as they escape their tunnels inundated by spring rains. Pull up a weed from the wet soil of the drenched garden and smell the rich life the earthworm has left behind. Just a whiff of it will flood you with a feeling of well-being. The microbes in freshly turned soil stimulate serotonin production, working on the human brain the same way antidepressants do.

Here is the world I need, a world that exists far beyond the impulse to scroll and scroll. The bluebird bringing pine straw to the nest box in a sunny spot of the yard, like the chickadee bringing moss to the box under the trees, is doing her work with the urgency of the ages. She has no care for me. Even her watchful mate ignores me as I dig in the flower bed beside our driveway.

The natural world's perfect indifference has always been the best cure for my own anxieties. Every living thing—every bird and mammal and reptile and amphibian, every tree and shrub and flower and moss—is pursuing its own vital purpose, a purpose that sets my human concerns in a larger context. The dramas and worries and pain that are the warp of my life, woven tightly through the light and love and joy that are its weft, don't register on the blue jay at all. The earthworms beneath the soil haven't the least idea of the frets that pluck at my heart. In their rest, I find rest.

And the natural world is everywhere, not just in my wild yard, or on my favorite trail at the local park, or in the woods beside the borrowed cabin. It's in the branches of the sidewalk trees as they begin to split open and change the grayscape to green. It's in the sparrows and the starlings taking nesting materials into the cracks around the windows and doorways of commercial buildings. It's in a sky full of drifting clouds, and in the sandhill cranes flying beneath the clouds.

I can scroll and worry indoors, or I can step outside and remember how it feels to be part of something larger, something timeless, a world that reaches beyond me and includes me, too. The spring ephemerals have only the smallest window for blooming, and so they bloom when the sunlight reaches them. Once the forest becomes enveloped in green and the sunlight closes off again, they will wait for the light to come back.

Wildflowers at My Feet and Songbirds in My Trees

Spring ❧ Week 5

Nothing is so beautiful as Spring— / When weeds, in
wheels, shoot long and lovely and lush.

—GERARD MANLEY HOPKINS, "Spring"

The flowering trees—dogwoods and redbuds and serviceberries, crab apples and peaches and cherries—are in full
splendor now, and every time it rains, the streets are paved with
petals. But the flowers I love best are the tiny ones, invisible from
a car window. Exquisite flowers, most of them smaller than my
pinkie fingernail, bloom all around my house in April, and they
have wonderful names: woodland violet, spring beauty, daisy flea-
bane, pitcher's stitchwort, birdeye speedwell, yellow wood sorrel,
purple deadnettle, creeping Charlie, dandelion, and many others.
Something new every day. Most people call them weeds.

A few of these flowers aren't native to Tennessee, and some of
the non-natives can be invasive. Those I pull up, or Haywood
mows down, but the others are beneficial, early blooming wildflowers that pollinators need. Long before my actual pollinator
garden is lush with cultivated flowers, the flowers I didn't plant are

blooming, an ankle-high meadow thriving in the place where most Americans grow grass. Wildflower seeds are carried on the wind, on the coats of animals, and in the digestive tracts of birds. Anybody paying attention would see them for the gifts they are: flowers that arrive, through no effort, to feed the bees and the butterflies.

Suburbia isn't paying attention. Homeowners are still in thrall to a status symbol invented by English nobility. People enraptured with the idea of a lawn as a rolling carpet of grass, a green that remains green even during seasons when grass is supposed to be dormant, can't help but see these homely flowers as intruders.

They consider this question, if they consider it at all, as a matter of personal preference: I like wildflowers, and they like grass. But with biodiversity disappearing from every ecosystem on the planet, including our own, our preferences aren't ethically equal. Lawns are a waste of precious water and soil because non-native landscaping like turf grass and boxwoods and crepe myrtles and Yoshino cherry trees provide little habitat or food for native wildlife.

Worse, a manicured lawn requires many different poisons to maintain. The wind that carries wildflower seeds to my uncultivated yard also carries wildflower seeds to my neighbors' highly cultivated grass. It's not easy to pull all those weeds, so homeowners—or their lawn services—set out poisons that keep the seeds from germinating. Then they spray a different poison that kills any plants that germinate anyway. Still another poison kills the insects that eat the "desirable" plants. Yet another kills the field mice trying to survive in a place without fields.

And those poisons don't stay put. They end up in the air and the water. They end up in our bodies, linked to asthma, Alzheimer's, Parkinson's, autism, and several cancers. It kills me to think of my baby bluebirds hunting poisoned insects in the yard next door. It kills me to think of Cooper's hawks eating the poisoned bluebirds. Every time I see my neighbors' children rolling around on their poisoned lawns, absorbing into their skin and breathing into their lungs these dangerous endocrine disrupters, I have to work hard not to cry. So much life is imperiled by what is merely fashionable: a green lawn, a tidy yard. It makes me feel lonely to think about it.

Loneliness is on my mind a lot these days. Haywood and I are helping our younger sons find a new place to live, and I am taking the looming move harder than I expected. They are hoping to be on the other side of the river, near their older brother and his wife, and there is a symmetry to this arrangement that floods me with gratitude. They will take care of one another, I know. Waiting for the sound of a car pulling into the driveway will no longer keep me half awake at night. This is what Haywood and I have been working toward their whole lives. But the human heart can be flooded with gratitude and grief at once, and I mourn this change with a sorrow I can't fully explain. Perhaps it's somehow related to all the other losses surrounding me.

We tend to think of nature in terms of its resilience. A rat snake eats all the redbird babies, and the parents build another nest somewhere else and try again. A tree dies slowly in the forest, and woodland creatures make a feast of the insects that live in the deadwood. But just because we can't see something doesn't mean it isn't happening. We hear birds singing in springtime, and we assume that all is well. We are wrong. Our songbirds are dying, and the news is even worse for insects and amphibians: *apocalypse* is the word scientists most often use to describe what's happening to these species.

The poet Gerard Manley Hopkins knew something about the vulnerability of the natural world:

What would the world be, once bereft
Of wet and of wildness? Let them be left,
O let them be left, wildness and wet;
Long live the weeds and the wilderness yet

There's only so much one person can do. When I give in to
despair, when I have found a perfect Cooper's hawk lying dead on
a nearby lawn, or a field mouse panting in the middle of the street,
crazed by the poison killing it from inside, that's what I tell myself.
There's only so much I can do here, and it isn't very much. It's
hardly anything.

Then I watch the green sweat bees crawling across the dandelions and the bluebird bringing pine straw to the nest box. I hear
the honeybees working the spring beauties and the blue jay croon-
ing a whisper song to his mate and the first cricket tuning up on
the first warm evening. I wake in the morning to find that our resident rabbit has nibbled all the petals off the tickseed, and I am
thrilled. The flowers are for her. All the flowers are for her.

Praise Song for
the Killdeer on the
School Softball Field

We were reading Hopkins, and my students were puzzled. How could the world be bent? What did it mean that the Holy Ghost is brooding over the bent world?

"Can you think of any words that mean the same as 'bent'?" I asked.

"How is the Holy Ghost often portrayed in art?" I asked.

But these were city kids in a secular school. They had never heard of a brooding bird or seen a hen settle on a clutch of eggs. They had not been taught by nuns that in scripture the Holy Spirit sometimes appears as a dove. I demonstrated the way a bird can sit on fragile eggs without breaking them: the careful adjustment of world-shaped eggs, the embrace of sheltering wings.

"Oh, like that bird on the softball field," one student said, and so we had to go outside and see.

The student led us straight to a killdeer nesting on the ground, her speckled eggs nearly invisible in the outfield. The bird stood up in alarm as we approached, but when she saw that we would come no closer she settled again, exactly as Hopkins writes: "with warm breast and with ah! bright wings."

Metamorphosis

Spring ✤ Week 6

I n Alabama, the fallen leaves were full of toads. Walk in the
woods at dusk, and toads would spring from the path into the
underbrush, toad after toad with every step, like a marching band
synchronized with your steps, leading you into the gloaming. In
the garden, every carelessly tipped-over flowerpot became home to
a toad. In town, streetlights drew toads every night. I could not say
how many moths they consumed in the dark, or how many, many
mosquitoes, but come morning flattened toads lay in the road
beneath every light, and still toads came by the dozens the following night, too. Toads enough for the snakes and the owls and the
raccoons and the opossums and the skunks, toads enough for the
crows, and still enough toads left over to waste beneath the streetlights night after summer night.

The leaf litter was full of toads but also of spring peepers, those
thrilling, trilling, night-singing harbingers of spring. The trees
were full of tree frogs: green tree frogs and pine woods tree frogs
and Cope's gray tree frogs, and those were just the ones I knew by
name. The ponds were full of leopard frogs and pickerel frogs and
every kind of chorus frog. My God, the music! The bass-voiced

bullfrogs, of course, syncopated them all. In springtime, you could hardly hear yourself think for all the singing, and the birdbaths would sprout tadpoles overnight.

PICTURE, NOW, the girl I was in Alabama, and the boy my brother was, and consider that this was in the early 1970s, when no one entertained children or signed them up for games where adults set all the rules.

We are half feral, a boy and a girl left to our own devices for hour after hour in the shade-deep woods. Possibly we tell our mother where we are going, or possibly she knows she can find us at the creek if she needs us to come home early. She never needs us to come home early. A running creek in springtime calls to a child as irresistibly as it calls to any thirsty bird or hungry raccoon, as irresistibly as it calls to any wild creature looking for a watery place to lay her eggs.

Our favorites are the toads. You would not believe how soft a toad is to the touch—soft, soft, and so dry! Nothing like the way you'd think a toad would feel. I love the jutting toad elbows and the crouched toad knees and the splayed toad fingers and toes, all so dear, so similar to our own. We are gentle with the toads. They are as soft as a great-grandmother you can hold in your hand.

We decide one day to catch some tadpoles and bring them indoors. The old aquarium with the crack in one wall was my brother's, back when it was still an aquarium, and maybe that's why we put the tank in his room and not mine. We set a cereal bowl at one end and fill it with creek water and pebbles. We swirl in some algae. That's where the tadpoles will live. Then we add dirt to the rest of the tank until it is level with the bowl's rim. Just for variety, or maybe because Billy knows it will be pretty, we add more dirt and create a slope down to the cereal-bowl pond. On the slope we place whatever small woodland plants we can gather, roots and all: violets and moss and some kind of fern. I am not interested in the plants—or, it must be said, in beauty—but Billy is an artist, and he arranges the plants around a piece of slate that he cantilevers into the soil at an angle, the way it would be found in the world itself.

We gather two minuscule tadpoles in a jelly jar full of creek water. Carefully we pour them into the cereal bowl. Their mother laid long strings of black eggs in the backwash of the creek, literally thousands of eggs, but we aren't greedy. One tadpole friend each is all we take. Mine is a little bit bigger than my brother's—that's how we can tell them apart.

Every day the tadpoles grow, and one day wee legs sprout from the soft black egg that is my tadpole's body. A few days later, the other tadpole grows legs, too. Before long, there are two pairs of legs each. As the tadpoles grow, their tails shorten, and that's the way it goes for weeks: smaller and smaller tails, larger and more powerful legs.

Eventually a minuscule toad climbs out of the water and sits on the soil, looking exactly like a full-grown toad but smaller than a shirt button. Soon a second toad emerges. We can hardly believe it. Apart from adding fresh algae and more water from time to time, we have done nothing to help them, and yet here they are all the same, perfect. We name them, of course, but the names we invent are too foolish to tell.

Now we have a problem: what to feed these miniature creatures? We start with roly-polies, which are plentiful and easy to catch—all you have to do is turn over any rock in the yard or any brick edging the flowerbed. The baby toads eat them up, even though the roly-polies are nearly as large as they are.

To watch a toad eat a roly-poly is a remarkable thing. You set the roly-poly down, and at first it just lies there, rolled up, a pebble, a marble, a pill. But soon enough the doomed creature feels safe and sets about exploring its violet-bedecked home. The roly-poly is marching along on its translucent legs, minding its own business, and that's when the toad spies it. The toad turns, and now it is oriented straight toward the roly-poly, a toadly Earth to the roly-poly's moon.

One hop takes the toad closer. Another hop takes it closer still. Then, long before it is close enough to catch the roly-poly—you could swear it is not even *remotely* close enough to catch the roly-poly—something happens so fast you can't possibly see it, and then the roly-poly is gone. I mean, it is just *gone*.

In that manner, the toads attain a certain amount of heft, growing from button-sized to thimble-sized, and now we begin to run out of roly-polies. We try ants and we try slugs, and the toads are happy with the ants and the slugs, but slugs are disgusting to pick up, and ants bite. Crickets are harder to catch, but crickets are bigger, so we don't need as many. Crickets are also harder for the toads to catch, it turns out, and that makes it seem somehow fairer to the one of us who is more tender-hearted. You may be able to guess by now which of us is the more tender-hearted.

And indeed it *is* fairer, for one morning Billy wakes up and looks into the aquarium-turned-terrarium, and crawling all across the soil are translucent baby crickets! Somehow a caught cricket has survived long enough to lay eggs, and now the eggs have hatched. The toads, impassive as always, are systematically scooping up baby crickets, but they cannot catch them all, and so, completely by accident, we have created a self-contained cricket-replenishing, toad-growing system.

The problem, it eventually becomes clear, is the growing. These are adult toads now, a good two inches end to end, but they are still living in an old ten-gallon aquarium on a table in my brother's room.

Perhaps you see where this is going.

First, a word about my brother's room. This is a time when we are living in a three-bedroom townhouse apartment. All the official bedrooms are upstairs—I have one bedroom, and our baby sister has one, and our parents have one. Billy sleeps in the small dining room, closed off from the front door by a sheet of wood-grain paneling nailed to the wall, and from the kitchen by a curtain mounted in the doorway on a spring rod.

Here is how we learn that the toads can get out of the old aquarium and find their way into the kitchen: early one morning, before it is quite light outdoors, we hear our mother scream.

Now you know how Dotodo and Otodo ended up back in the woods, near the backwash of the creek where they first hatched. (And now you also know why I hesitated to tell you their names.) Whatever happened to them after that happened in the world beyond our sight, but we believed they were fine. In those days there were still so many crickets in the woods, and the woods went on forever.

The years since then have turned into decades, and I never see a toad anymore. Back in Alabama, the woods where we played became a strip mall and even more apartment buildings. In the neighborhood where I live now in Nashville there is still a patch of woods left behind the last few houses before the dead end, but a toad's soft skin is vulnerable to chemicals, and I am not surprised they cannot survive here. I miss the toads. In spring, especially, I miss the toads.

But there are tree frogs here, a few, and I can hear them singing after every long summer rain. Sometimes they take up a spot in a particular driveway culvert down the street, and there their singing echoes in a new timbre. I worry about them, though, clinging to the wall of the culvert. That's where the lawn poisons concentrate after a rain.

And so my youngest son and I went to a farm-supply store, bought a forty-gallon stock tank, and set it under a tree in a shady part of the yard. We have no cattle or sheep or goats with a need for drinking water, but the neighborhood has frogs in need of habitat. We have filled the stock tank and ordered a few water plants that grow naturally in this part of the world. In time this poor man's pond will collect twigs and fallen leaves, and the leaves will molder and make of this place a haven for tadpoles. I don't know how long it will take the tree frogs to find the nursery we've built for them, but I have faith they will. This faith wavers and often fades, but what else do I have to offer anymore? Faith sometimes feels like the very last thing I've got.

Praise Song for
the Alien in the Shade Garden

It appears overnight, nestled among the fern's jagged fronds: a ruddy head on a ruddy stem, two ruddy fists clenched just above the place where a heart would be. The small face is bowed, as in defeat. In fear. It appears to be full of doubt. Has it landed on a hospitable planet, a habitable world? Early signs are not favorable.

But warmth will coax it to release its tight grip. Light will loosen its beauty, one serrated frond at a time. Warmth and light will call it here. Into the place where it belongs.

Hide and Seek

Spring ❧ Week 7

In the green morning / I wanted to be a heart. / A heart.

—FEDERICO GARCÍA LORCA, "Ditty of First Desire"

Tennessee's Lost Cove, a hidden nook on the Cumberland Plateau, is one of the most biodiverse tracts of land in this country. Its more than five thousand acres are home to some of the last remnants of virgin forest on the Plateau—oak, hickory, maple, buckeye, tulip poplar, sourwood, basswood—and a number of rare plants, including some that grow nowhere else. It has long been a refuge for Haywood and me, too, but it became especially beloved during the pandemic: a place where we could be alone, a way to give our sons some time away from us.

When we borrow our friends' cabin, we fill their birdfeeders and sit in their porch rocking chairs. We watch vultures and hawks riding thermals in the sky. Haywood keeps hoping to explore the trackless cove someday, but I worry about stepping on a fragile, irreplaceable snail or lady's slipper. I am content to sit on the porch and listen to the crows calling to one another from the tops of trees so tall it's impossible to see them among the branches.

Like the rest of Tennessee, the Plateau is now stricken by regular droughts, and my friend is always concerned about the birds. "Please keep an eye out for the pileated woodpeckers while you're there," she will text before we head up the mountain. "I haven't seen one since the drought. I'm worried."

Often there is no sign of a pileated, but on one visit in the midst of the breeding season, I heard their unmistakable cry. I was determined to get a picture to send as kind of a thank-you gift, but the bird kept eluding me. Pileated woodpeckers are gigantic, one of the biggest birds in the deciduous forest, and they have distinctive red crests, too. How hard could it be to find one when I could hear it perfectly plainly?

Very hard.

I began to leave the dog on the porch while I searched, though Rascal is offended at the very idea of being left behind when I am heading into a forest full of intoxicating scents.

For three days, I walked up and down the nearby paths, several times a day, without so much as a glimpse of my quarry. Then, early one morning, I startled a woodpecker busy yanking big hanks of wood out of a long-downed tree. In an instant, before I could register anything more than his unmistakable red crest, he was airborne. With a kind of stupid awe, I watched him fly away. Absorbed by the grace of his undulating flight, I never thought to reach for my camera.

This will make me sound like the worst sort of crank, but here is the truth: the only reason I carry a cell phone is to have a camera in my pocket, ready to record something extraordinary. I can't see the point of taking selfies. This pronouncement is surely an irony coming from an essayist, someone who keeps her finger on her own pulse for a living. As a writer, I err toward earnestness, but I'm at ease with this particular irony. The visible world is astonishingly, heartbreakingly lovely. Why waste it looking at myself?

On the other hand, what good is having a camera in your pocket if you don't take it out in the presence of something wild and beautiful and rare? I stood that morning, motionless, while the most primeval of all the woodland birds disappeared into the forest. I walked out of the woods with not a single image to commemorate the encounter.

I was angry with myself, trudging back toward the cabin, but it wasn't long before I began to reconsider. Even when it is pointed in the right direction, a camera has a way of stunting sight. How truly valuable is a device that makes you take your eyes from an experience so momentary you might miss it altogether? I saw a magnificent pileated woodpecker that day in the woods. I am grateful I didn't miss it.

While I stood there, stunned, my camera still in my pocket, a group of whitetail deer galloped through the trees at a full run, close enough for me to see their bobbing tails go by but so well disguised I had no idea of their number. And darting among the golden seed clusters at the tops of the elms, goldfinches were feasting, so exactly matched to the flowers that I never saw a single bird. I didn't need my camera—I knew them by their call.

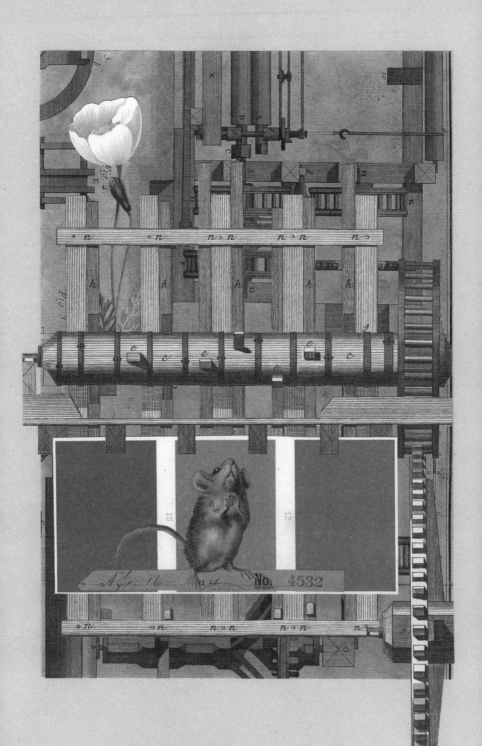

No. 4532

My Life in Mice

Spring ✤ Week 8

> It begins to make me dizzy even trying to think of taking
> a census of everybody who lives here; and all of them seem
> to have certain claims to the place that are every bit as
> good as and perhaps better than mine.
>
> —SUE HUBBELL, *A Country Year*

Mouse (1971)

The apartment is new, the first to be finished in an entire complex of buildings being carved out of a pine forest. In daytime the site is full of construction workers, and the air rings with the sound of saws and hammers and drills. Only my family is here at night. At night the woods echo with clicks and buzzes and screams, but I am a girl who is brave. This is what everyone tells me.

I steal downstairs with my flashlight and my Nancy Drew book. Looking for cookies, I swing the beam across the shelves in the pantry. Something is stirring in the cracker box. Something is making the cracker box shiver on the shelf. But how? The box is new, its flaps sealed.

Now *I* am the girl detective. I set the box on the floor and squat to break open the flaps, tear past the wax-coated paper.

The flashlight I hold under my chin catches the gleaming black eyes of a mouse, hugely pregnant, perched on her hind legs and holding a cracker in her hands, utterly still. I jump back, catching myself on the heels of my hands and dropping the flashlight. The mouse leaps, kicks, bolts past me. I feel her feet on the back of my hand. I grab the flashlight, but she's gone. Now the beam reveals a small round hole in the back of the box, like a bull's-eye. Hardly big enough for me to wiggle my finger through.

Guinea Pig (1973)

The family next door has a pet guinea pig who lives under their dishwasher. When I babysit, the neighbors tell me to wait till the children are asleep before giving the guinea pig his supper. They say I don't need to whistle when I shake pellets into his shallow bowl, or even when I set out a leaf of spinach—the guinea pig knows the rattle of his own food container and also the sound of the human refrigerator door being opened. The neighbors don't tell me why the guinea pig lives under their dishwasher, but I know these children very well, and I can guess the reasons why this soft, murmuring creature has made its home in a hidden place, far out of reach.

Squirrel (1976)

Sent to the back steps to shell pecans for a pie, I toss the wormy nuts into the yard, thinking to feed any creatures who are less picky than we are about eating unblemished nuts. It's a small yard, and the nearby animals appear to have their doubts about descending from the trees while a human sits on the steps. None of the blue jays and none of the crows will come so close, not even for a delicacy like pecans. The raccoon, of course, will wait for nightfall to look for the nuts I'm discarding.

Then one squirrel, bolder than the others, moves gingerly down the nearest pine tree, pausing to shake his tail from time to time. I stop. He stops. He shakes his tail. He stops again, waiting to see if I am about to move. I don't move. Finally, in a rush, he dashes for a nut, turns in a blur, and dashes back to the tree.

It will be years before I understand why I shouldn't feed wild animals, and I am delighted by this bold squirrel. Every day after school I sit on the steps and toss nuts to him. When I realize that he will always carry unshelled pecans back up the tree to eat in safety, I begin to shell the nuts for him myself, tossing him only the meats. Soon he sees that he will have more to eat if he stays on the ground with me.

As the afternoons pass, I toss the nuts closer. With each incremental change that narrows the space between us, he comes just a bit nearer. It is only a matter of days before he is taking nuts from my hand, leaning and stretching toward me, his feet spread wide and braced for an explosive escape, his tail a furious flag.

A day arrives when he sits in my lap to take nuts from me, and after that we are off to the races. He comes when I call the name I have given him. He follows me into the house to drink from the dog's water bowl. When spring comes, he nibbles my barefoot mother's toes while she is hanging clothes on the line, perhaps not entirely certain of the difference between human fingers and human toes.

But pecans are a cash crop in Lower Alabama. The generous supply my grandparents have spared us from their orchard is dwindling, and Mama has figured out where her pecans are going. No more, she says. Pecans are too expensive to throw in the yard. I walk to the Piggly Wiggly, planning to use my babysitting money to buy more nuts, but babysitting wages are no match for grocery store prices. There will be no more nuts on my grandparents' trees till fall, and so there will be no more visits to the backyard after school, for I cannot come empty-handed. In time the squirrel who was my friend is my friend no longer.

Mouse (1980)

I am homesick, but I am also animal-sick. I can hardly bear to be so far from my dog and my lovebird, but pets aren't allowed in the dorm. I consider trying to sneak the bird into my room anyway, but he is very, very loud, and he would not be a secret for long. On my first trip home for the weekend, I buy a feeder mouse to keep in Otodo and Dotodo's old aquarium, plus shavings to fill it with, and bring the mouse back to school with me. While I write out my Latin exercises, she explores my desk, chasing the pencil tip across my notebook. While I sleep, she runs in her wheel. She is exactly what I need. After she eats, she climbs into the palm of my hand and washes her face by licking her paws and running them carefully across her mouth, first one side and then the other.

Rat (1987)

The man I will marry has an old friend who lives in a cabin for most of the year. In winter he travels from tree farm to tree farm, planting pines. It is winter, and I am not planting trees. I am studying for the comprehensive exams I must take in springtime, and I am growing more anxious by the day. "Let's borrow Starr's cabin for the weekend," Haywood says. "It will do you good to get to the woods, and no one will bother you while you study."

Cabin, it turns out, is something of a misnomer. I have been picturing a tidy woodland cottage in a sunny clearing, a storybook cabin with window boxes and flower beds, but this makeshift structure is more of a piece with the forest itself. No water. No heat. Gaps where the wind whistles through. Quilts are piled high on our friend's bed, and there is a stack of wood next to the fireplace. The fireplace is rough-hewn, with no grate to prevent popping sparks from landing on the bed. "Wake me up if you hear anything," the unworried man I will marry says before turning over to sleep. "We don't want a burning log to roll out of the fireplace."

While he sleeps, I hear everything. I hear the barred owls courting in the trees outside. I hear the trees themselves creaking in the wind and the scuttle of dry leaves drifting across the ground. Nothing I hear is a log rolling out of the fireplace. Finally, I fall asleep myself.

The sound that wakes me is a stirring inside the cabin, the rush and rustle of furtive feet. I sit up in bed and peer at the fire, which has died down to embers. Backlit by the glow, a rat crosses the hearth. Another rat sits up on the stack of firewood, its teacup ears pink and translucent. Each whisker ends in a point of light. It lifts its nose, testing the night, trying to decide what to make of me in my quilts, also sitting up, also watching from the shadows.

Hamster v. Gerbil (2000)

The gerbils live peacefully together in one glass tank, but the grouchy hamster is a solitary creature and lives alone. "It's fine to take them out," Haywood cautions the babysitter, "but don't try to play with the hamster while the gerbils are out. They don't get along."

Perhaps the babysitter isn't listening. Perhaps she hears but doesn't understand. Perhaps she is distracted by our children, rambunctious in their parents' absence, when she drops one of the gerbils into the aquarium where the hamster lives.

Hours later, after I have driven the babysitter home and we have settled into bed, we hear an unfamiliar noise. It is coming from our firstborn's room: a frantic scrambling. When Haywood goes to check, he finds the hamster tank rattling on the bookcase. Blood is smeared on the glass. In the corner sits a battered gerbil poised to spring, panting.

That's the moment when I decide: never again will we keep a creature in a cage.

Praise Song for the Redbird Who Has Lost His Crest and the Skink Who Has Lost His Tail

I don't know why the redbird lost his finery months out of time, but the skink has clearly made a timely getaway, snatching his own life from the jaws (or the claws, or the beak) of lurking death. Was it a hungry crow who grabbed him by the tail? A silent owl? A wily fox leaping in the dusk? I will never know. I will watch as his tail grows back, a miracle of regeneration, just as I will watch the bald redbird grow new feathers in August, when the molting season comes around again. His poor skull is an unsightly gray these days, but he has not lost most of his boastful colors, any more than the tailless skink has lost his flame-red face, the color of the breeding season. Renewal is a costly effort, exhausting and uncomfortable, but these creatures are going about the work of springtime with all their usual fervor. The skink's mate has gone off to lay her eggs, as she always does, and already the redbird is feeding babies in the holly tree. I hear them calling him. I see him returning with a juicy moth to offer the loudest one. The one who will not wait.

The Bobcat Next Door

Spring ❧ Week 9

> I have never lived a moment not yearning to undo the damage.
>
> —JANISSE RAY, *Wild Spectacle*

One fine spring morning the dog and I came across a female pileated woodpecker pulling chunks of wood out of a stump in a neighbor's yard. The dog froze, arrested by the sight of this giant bird, but the bird paid us no mind. She was focused on the stump in that intense, almost animatronic way of pileateds. I hurried the dog home and came back in the car, figuring I would be less apt to startle her with my camera if the lens was at least partially obscured. Even the most human-habituated birds tend to flee when they're pointed at, and I have never known a pileated woodpecker to become truly habituated to human presence. They are the very embodiment of wildness—pterodactyls clinging to the sugar maple trees.

I had taken several pictures, careful not to lean out the window, when the bird suddenly stopped her work and hopped to the top of the stump, poised to fly. I was still taking pictures, so I didn't figure out right away that I was not the one who had spooked her.

Finally, at the very edge of my viewfinder, I noticed two front legs, out of focus from the difference in depth of field. I looked up expecting to see a large dog attached to those legs.

It took a moment for my own field of vision to adjust, for my mind to fit the unexpected pieces together:

Stunted tail.

Spotted legs.

Lean, feline flank.

Muscled shoulders.

Eyespots on pointed ears.

Fangs.

Fangs?

I gasped. It was a full-grown bobcat. In broad daylight. I had never seen such a magnificent animal in the wild. I've seen red foxes and coyotes and great horned owls and rat snakes and opossums and at least one massive raccoon. But even my backyard trail camera has not found evidence of a bobcat.

The cat stalked across the front of the house. The woodpecker watched every measured step, swiveling on the stump when the cat took a hard right at the property line. She flew away only when the cat was parallel with the stump, hardly more than one bobcat-leap away.

I, on the other hand, just sat there. Unmoving. Disbelieving. It was nine o'clock on a sunny spring morning, and a bobcat was calmly walking to the edge of the yard and crossing the street, right in front of my car.

When it reached the other side of the street, it disappeared behind some bushes, following the dry creek bed that channels runoff after rainstorms. That route would take the cat to a culvert beneath the main road that runs along the edge of our neighborhood. The culvert leads into a little wooded area on the other side of the main road—those woods were once slated for a commercial development before neighbors hastily arranged for a zoning change to prevent it—and from there to a twelve-month wet creek. Following the bobcat's likely path in my mind, I realized that the creek leads to and from many other creeks that crisscross this water-threaded town. Once it was safely out of our neighborhood, the cat would be following what amounts to a wildlife corridor through the heart of Nashville.

Still, I sent a photo to a wildlife rescue center to ask if I should be concerned that this famously secretive creature was so openly walking around our suburban neighborhood. It's rarely a good idea to relocate a wild animal—they are nearly always safer in their own territories, where they know the food and water sources, the hiding places, the opportunities to nest or den up—but this bobcat had me worried. Should I get the state wildlife agency involved?

Absolutely not, the expert at the rescue center wrote back. "Wildlife species we usually don't associate with suburbia can actually thrive in places where we live, particularly highly adaptable species like bobcats. This one does look to be a very healthy adult, so it would definitely be best to let it be."

I never saw the bobcat again, but friends on the other side of the main road have seen it. Haywood has seen it twice. It seems to be thriving. There are fewer rabbits in the neighborhood.

And Then There Were None

Spring ✤ *Week 10*

The spring migration's first rose-breasted grosbeak was sitting quietly on the tray feeder where I leave whole peanuts for the blue jays. The grosbeak had come from his wintering grounds in Central or South America, and he arrived apparently too tired to cling to the tube feeder I'd filled with safflower seeds specifically for the grosbeak migration. After he moved again to the safety of the trees, I got up to shake some safflower seeds into the tray feeder to help him recover from his long journey, to help him fuel up for the long journey still ahead.

On the other side of the house, a pair of bluebirds was feeding their lone chick in the nest box I put up years ago. They were veteran parents—the female laid six eggs, too large a clutch for a first-timer, and the male was vigilant about protecting the nest. He had lived long enough to know the risks to his young. Even so, there was just one baby bluebird left in the nest by the time the grosbeak arrived, though only a week earlier there had been two.

I spent a lot of time that spring wondering what happened to those other eggs, what happened to that missing nestling. Did the first eggs freeze in a cold snap before the last eggs appeared? Did a predator carry them off and come back later for one of the young? Did the baby die from some other cause, and did its own parents pull the body from the nest?

I will almost certainly never know, just as I won't know the fate of the exhausted rose-breasted grosbeaks who stay here for only a day or two before moving on.

To pay close attention to the natural world is to exist in medias res. Life is an unfolding that responds to the cues of seasonal change, but for our purposes it is also suspended in an everlasting present. We can see some of the creatures we share our world with, or at least some evidence of their nearness, but we cannot know the full arc of their story. Every encounter in the outdoors is an episode with a cliffhanger ending.

In the wild, we see either the story's vulnerable beginning, or its territorial middle, or its heartbreaking end, but we almost never see more than one of those stages for an individual. We are storytelling animals, and for us that indeterminate space is uncomfortable. We turn the unfinished story over and over in our minds, imagining alternate scenarios. We try to convince ourselves that only the happy ending is possible, that any tragedies we fail to witness are tragedies that never happened. That kind of ignorance is a gift we give ourselves because we are made so uneasy by uncertainty.

But uncertainty is the true gift. I know this because after there were six eggs, and after there were two nestlings, and after there was one, there were none. I know this because I know what happened to that last lone bluebird chick.

I killed him.

I was trying to save his life, though that is no excuse. I know better than to interfere. I *know* better. Except when something unnatural is happening within a natural system—when a beagle grabs a baby rabbit, say, or an opossum gets caught in the crawl space—it's always best to let nature take its course, no matter how distressing its course might be. When the rat snake climbed the downspout and entered the chickadee nest a few years ago, I did not intervene, even hearing the parents trying so hard and so fruitlessly to chase the snake away. It haunts my dreams, but I did not save those baby birds.

But when the lone bluebird chick left the nest far too early and I found him on the ground, days before he would be old enough to fly, I didn't know what to do. I knew his parents would continue to care for him, and I knew that under normal circumstances they would do a better job than I ever could. But I found him there, camouflaged in the sun-dappled weeds, by watching a feral cat stalking one of his parents, who was clearly trying to distract it from a baby bird that *should* be tucked away in a wooden nest box for many more days. And a cat is not part of the natural order of any ecosystem.

I wish I had never seen that cat. I wish I had never reached beneath that bright-eyed, blue-gray speck of fluff and lifted him gently into my hand. I wish I hadn't opened the door to the nest box and set him back inside. More than anything, I wish the baby bird had not chosen the exact moment when I shut the door to leap again, had not been caught between one wall and the other.

And oh, how desperately I wish I had not been there to watch the life go out of his eyes.

Dust to Dust

Spring ✢ Week 11

> For the growing good of the world is partly dependent on
> unhistoric acts; and that things are not so ill with you and
> me as they might have been, is half owing to the number
> who lived faithfully a hidden life, and rest in unvisited
> tombs.

—George Eliot, *Middlemarch*

R ural children have graveyards instead of playgrounds. That
was true when I was growing up, at least, visiting my grandparents in Lower Alabama. A graveyard is hallowed ground, but
holiness means little to children. To them a cemetery is the ideal
playspace—a grassy, tree-shaded park offering objects to climb on
and jump from, dirt to dig in, things to throw at other children.
(Magnolia seedpods were pressed into service as imaginary gre-
nades by many a Southern boy during my Vietnam War–era childhood.) I was past childhood before I learned that I was supposed
to be frightened in graveyards. Nothing has ever worried me about
the places where the unknown dead lie beneath the soil.

It is coming on June now, the time last year when my
father-in-law began to fail, and then failed very quickly, and I am
stunned to be thinking again of death while all this *life* surrounds

me. The hummingbirds are back from their long journey. The wild geraniums are blooming beside daisies covered with iridescent sweat bees. How can an irreplaceable life end in the midst of so many beginnings?

Often it happens this way, and I know it. I lost my own mother in less than twenty-four hours on another day in another June. The way death and life mingle and tangle, like the passion vine that twines among the blackberry canes in my pollinator garden—it's always been like that. Or maybe it's only death itself that comes as a shock, a giant rent in the tightly woven shroud we wear without noticing for all our days, no matter how many or how few we are given.

My father-in-law was born the same year as my father, but he survived Dad by close to two decades. He was my father-in-law for nearly as many years as my father was my father. Death at ninety-two should not be a surprise, but months later I can still be startled by reminders that my father-in-law is gone. At the store, I pause in the ice cream aisle before remembering that we no longer need to keep ice cream in the house to delight a loved one with so few delights left. I open the nest box to photograph the baby bluebirds, and then I remember that there is no reason to take pictures. For so long my father-in-law was too feeble to stand on tiptoe and peek into the box himself, but he always wanted to know about the baby birds.

There is a barrier island on the Georgia coast where Haywood's family has buried their dead for generations. White settlers first altered that landscape more than four hundred years ago, but the island remained a wildlife sanctuary by default, sparsely populated and difficult to reach. Then came the first bridge.

More than a thousand acres of coastal marsh and maritime forest are still protected, but now a causeway funnels vacationers to and from the mainland, and the island is packed cheek by jowl with grand summer homes and high-rise condos, all booked months in advance. Those vacationers are the reason we could not lay my father-in-law's ashes to rest beside my mother-in-law's until months after his death: all the rental housing was taken.

Shaded by live oak trees draped with Spanish moss, the island graveyard is very different from the cemeteries of my childhood, but when we finally arrived with my father-in-law's ashes, it brought the old places back to me just the same. I felt at home there, just as I feel at home in any quiet country churchyard with wind-rustled leaves and singing mockingbirds and tilting tombstones, the kind of cemetery where grass grows right on top of the graves. They remind me of the beloved place in Lower Alabama where I played hide-and-seek, where life and death come together in a way that isn't possible in the burial grounds of more prosperous people. The peace of the dead, verdant and timeless, invites many animals to make their homes there. And children, poking about with far more patience than adults would believe, can easily find these secret homes.

If a rabbit's nest is hidden next to the gray granite of a monument, the grass above it will be dry and shading to brown.

Look for the squirrel's drey in the crook of the oak limb, and you will hear a faint rustling within the ball of brown leaves carefully tucked among the green ones.

The hole that opens up next to the chokecherry roots might be where a groundhog has gone to ground. Pretend to walk away and then creep back. A groundhog is too curious not to wonder where you've gone, and soon a wrinkling black nose and lively eyes will present themselves, if only for an instant.

There is no mistaking the location of the mockingbird's nest in the dense holly hedge, though you see nothing of it, for the mockingbird will dive at you with murder in his eye if you venture near his family.

This place belongs not to the bones lying underground but to everything that death feeds—the soil, the beetles, the baby crows teetering on the edge of the high nest, urging themselves to fly on untested wings. Is this why I love graveyards so much, after all, and not the happy memories of hide-and-seek among the stones? Because they are so very filled with life? Within their rusted iron gates, life is protected in ways that the built world fails to provide almost everywhere else.

My husband's parents are together again now, as near in death as they were in life for more than sixty years. Their headstones are paired in the way that I still think of them: side by side. After so many years with Haywood, I know their family stories as well as I know my own parents'. But beyond what is carved into the granite markers, almost nothing is known today about the people who lie beneath the oldest stones. A name, a set of dates—perhaps only one date, from a time when birth years weren't recorded or even known. The rare bit of extra information might be the word *Mother*. Whose mother? Unless the names on nearby stones give a hint, those kinships are lost to time. Green, hallowed, belonging to human history. Belonging to the wild future. To our future, too.

Praise Song for
Solomon's Seal

The purple-tinged stalks pop out of the ground with their foliage tightly furled, but very soon the leaves will open up like a teenager who has learned she's beautiful, like a lonely person finally loved. The striped leaves are all you notice at first, the perfect embodiment of springtime: cool and green and growing. Then, in a day or two, the white flowers appear, dainty and delicate, miniature bells nodding toward the damp soil on purple stems, nearly hidden under the showy leaves.

Bend down. Lean closer. The flowers will stir in the wake of your smallest breath. These bells are ringing for anyone who listens to the rustle of wind in the leaves, to the hush of sweat bees moving from flower to flower in the cool spring air.

"Set me as seal upon your heart, as a seal upon your arm," the poet says in the Song of Solomon, "for love is strong as death." Here is this profusion of flowers for proof.

An Acolyte of Benign Neglect

Spring ✤ Week 12

> That world is fast disappearing. But it's not gone yet.
>
> —WENDY WILLIAMS, *The Language of Butterflies*

I was pretty proud of myself the spring I planted my first garden. It was 1986, and I was a first-year graduate student. After six months in a city where I had no car and so no way to escape to the woods, I was desperate for nature, any kind of nature, and nature wasn't especially forthcoming at my garage apartment behind the Family Dollar store. But the Family Dollar sold seed packets, and I figured I'd give gardening a try. Surely the butterflies would find it, even so near a busy four-lane highway.

Growing up, I hadn't paid a lot of attention to my mother's passion for gardening, though paying attention would not have helped with my own plans: Mom believed in wiping out all insects with a liberal application of Sevin Dust, while I aimed for a strictly organic operation. In my garden, I would rely on companion planting—marigolds between the tomato vines, petunias beside the beans, sunflowers among the cucumbers—to repel bugs the natural way. Any lingering pests would be dispatched by beneficial insects like ladybugs and praying mantises.

One evening a few weeks after planting, I watched happily as cabbage white butterflies flitted over silvery broccoli leaves. Those little butterflies pausing on the water-beaded plants made for a charming tableau of bucolic harmony behind the Family Dollar.

It didn't dawn on me until the caterpillars appeared that a) those cabbage white butterflies had been carrying out the usual biological imperative of springtime, b) the butterfly's name references not only its color but also its host plant, and c) broccoli belongs to the cabbage family. Instead of broccoli, it turns out, I was raising cabbage white butterflies.

As their offspring turned those lovely, silvery plants into leafy lace, I ordered some praying mantis eggs from a catalog. No baby mantises ever emerged from the sac. I considered ordering live ladybugs next, but by then broccoli season was over and I was having better luck with tomatoes and peppers. Eventually I stopped trying to sort the damaging insects from the "beneficial" ones and started planting enough vegetables for all of us. Decades later, I gave up raising vegetables altogether and planted a pollinator garden. I was always rooting for the butterflies anyway.

Now my raised beds are full of native perennials that provide nectar for bees, wasps, skippers, and butterflies, or that serve as their nurseries: yarrow for painted lady butterflies, dill and parsley for black swallowtails, false indigo for clouded sulphurs, passion vine for gulf fritillaries, asters for pearl crescents, ironweed for American ladies. Most of all, I planted milkweed—butterfly weed and swamp milkweed, the varieties that fare best in this sun-limited yard—because milkweed is the host plant of the monarch butterfly, and the monarch is in danger of extinction. In a contest for garden space, the broccoli I can buy at the grocery store for $1.99 a pound carries no weight against the mass extinction of a butterfly once so numerous it filled the skies with gold.

Monarchs are the only butterfly known to conduct an extravagant multigenerational migration, flying thousands of miles north in the springtime and thousands of miles south in the fall. Somehow, butterflies that hatch in Minnesota and New York know how to get to their wintering grounds in Mexico without ever having left Minnesota or New York before. Along the way, there are many deadly assaults on the monarch population—herbicides, development, extreme weather—but the only one I have any power over is loss of habitat. I can't change Americans' love affair with poison, and I can't solve the problems of climate change, but I can plant a garden.

It takes the monarch four generations, sometimes more, to complete its annual migration. Each generation flies farther north to lay its eggs before the "Methuselah" generation turns south again and heads to Mexico. What those northbound butterflies need is milkweed, the only plant monarch caterpillars can eat. So I filled my garden with milkweed—more and more and more milkweed—and waited.

But years passed and not a single monarch arrived. Short of cutting down all our trees and replacing them with an entire field of milkweed, there was nothing more I could do. I finally decided to take the same approach to my pollinator garden that I had once adopted for my vegetables: I watered and I weeded, after a fashion, but mostly I let it go its own way.

Then one Sunday afternoon, I was reading a book on our back deck when a flash of orange in the pollinator garden caught my eye. From a distance it could be mistaken for a monarch, but from a distance *any* orange butterfly can be mistaken for a monarch. Years of roundly rejected milkweed had taught me my lesson.

Still, could it be?

I got up to look. There, lifting herself barely above the green leaves of the butterfly weed, was a female monarch, pale and tattered, looking as though she had come a great distance. She was fluttering from plant to plant, completely ignoring the nectar-filled flowers and pausing lightly on one milkweed leaf after another. When I looked closely, I could see she was laying eggs.

Five days later, the eggs hatched. It took a magnifying glass to be sure, but there they were: on each leaf an infinitesimal creature with black-and-yellow stripes and black faces and black waving antennae. By the time I found them, they were already eating, leaving behind pinprick-sized holes in the leaves.

Praise Song for
All the Beginnings

Precious, irreplaceable things pass away, often in a paroxysm of suffering, but life is stubborn, life is undeterred, and for every ending there are a thousand, a million beginnings.

When my mother died, I peeled away the soft white hair I found in her brush and put it in the antique powder jar that my grandmother used as a hair receiver. I kept it for a long time. For just an instant, if I opened the jar, I could remember my mother's scent.

The year it didn't smell like her anymore, I draped the skein of white hair across a holly branch. The pointed edges of the leaves held it safe until a chickadee claimed it for her nest.

The Grief of Lost Time

Spring ❧ Week 13

"I'll tell you this for free," said Crow.

—MAX PORTER, *Grief Is the Thing with Feathers*

D riving due south in spring is like speeding up time. My mother believed that the growing season expands northward at the rate of a hundred miles per week. I thought about her theory as I was driving south, watching new-green leaves fast-forward into a denser, deeper verdure. I had set off from Nashville in springtime, but when I arrived at my sister's house near Birmingham, it was already full summer.

I think about my parents every day, but there's something about watching the hardwood forests of Tennessee give way to the pineywoods of Alabama that brings them back to me with a fresh aching. Perhaps it's the pine trees that trigger the longing—straight and tall, lining the highway like a giant guardrail, shunting me in the right direction, a marble on a downhill track. But maybe it's only the familiar landscape itself, rolling where it should roll and sprawling where it should sprawl, that makes me feel I am somehow home.

I hadn't planned to make the trip. Spring is always such a busy time that I'd stuck Post-it notes all around my house reminding me to *Say no to everything*. But then a dear childhood friend texted to say her father had died, and I would not have missed his funeral for the world.

When I got to my sister's house that night, plans were in full swing for my nephew's high school graduation. As an emblem of passing time, it's hard to choose between an old man's funeral and a child's graduation. The night that child came home from the hospital, my job was to take him to his mother when he was hungry and put him down to sleep when he was full, but instead I stayed up all night marveling at all that life so neatly packaged in such a small person. All I did was turn my back for a second, half a second, and he was grown.

The next morning there was time before the funeral to wander around my sister's neighborhood, the same neighborhood we moved to when I was in eighth grade and she was in second, the same neighborhood where our father had lived as an even younger child. I found the spot at the end of the road where rusted tracks emerged from the weeds, the exact place where my father had waited for his own father to step off the trolley after work. I stopped at the bridge over the creek where my eighth-grade boyfriend first held my hand. I named to myself all the neighbors who had once lived on our street, every one of them gone now, as a scent drifted on the air that I couldn't place. Then, finally: *gardenia!* It blooms in profusion in Birmingham but not at all in Nashville, where I have lived for decades.

On past visits, I've avoided the streets that led to our old house, the house we convinced our mother to sell because it was falling into ruin, but I wanted to see it this time. I hardly recognized it in its fresh paint, with its new shutters and cheerful window boxes.

Gone was the asbestos-shingle siding, replaced by clapboards. Gone were my mother's perennial border and the chokecherry tree whose roots had buckled the driveway for years. But the silver maple sapling that my brother and sister and I gave our parents to mark their silver anniversary—it towers over the house now, its leaves glinting in the breeze. I stood and listened to those trembling leaves for longer than anyone watching from inside would have understood. Time means something different to me now than it did when I was a girl sharing a bed with my baby sister in our room at the corner of the house.

During the funeral, when my friend spoke about her parents' long marriage, I thought of my own parents' long marriage. When she recalled her father's irrepressible pride in his children, I remembered my own father's irrepressible pride in his children. When she spoke of the way her father's love always overcame their differences, I thought of the way my father, too, accepted my reconsiderations of the worldview he had imparted to me as a birthright.

In her eulogy, my friend reminded us of how much her father had loved to sail: "He always said that he felt at peace when sailing, where it was serene and quiet," she said. "I now appreciate that he enjoyed those days on the boat because the family was together without being in a hurry."

Instantly I was thinking about those Post-it notes stuck all over my house. How had I allowed myself to become so busy? How long had it been since I'd spent a day in the sun, eating sandwiches from a cooler and watching water ripple across the surface of a lake? Why do I so often behave as though there will be unlimited days to sit quietly with my own beloveds, listening to birdsong and wind in the pines?

A child who grew up playing in graveyards ought to grow up understanding the reach of mortality, the way it is always hurtling toward us faster than spring turns into summer on a southbound highway. Faster than a sapling becomes a shade tree and a house becomes someone else's home. Faster than a newborn baby becomes a man. And yet I conduct my life as though I have all the time in the world, filling my hours in ways I can't always account for when evening falls.

Leaving the funeral, I found myself thinking of my mother's last days. She was a lifelong gardener, but working the soil had become difficult, so I found a carpenter to build two raised beds, each waist high, next to the back porch of the rental house across the street from us in Nashville, where she lived during her final years. She stooped to dig in the dirt anyway.

After her sudden death, I found a holly fern in a plastic grocery bag on the porch. She'd dug it up from our old yard while she was staying with my sister the week before she died, and her trowel was stuck in the ground right where she must have planned to plant it. She didn't know it would not have lived through a Nashville winter. I took it home and put it in a pot.

Driving back from Alabama I kept thinking about that potted holly fern, about the way my mother had pulled it from the soil of the house where I spent my last years at home, about how I carry it inside every fall and outside every spring, year after year without thinking, as though the years are nothing, as though springtime will always be waiting for me, dappling everything with light.

Praise Song for
the Baby Chickadees

Something ate all five bluebird eggs, and something ate all three red-bird nestlings, but the Carolina chickadees finally raised four healthy babies in the nest box under the eaves, and their voices were like bells that changed in timbre with each passing day, moving down the register until their demands for food sounded almost exactly like the scolding beep-beep-beep their parents make when a bigger bird dares to visit the feeder they have claimed as their own. Then one morning I woke to silence, right on schedule, and they were all gone. It breaks my heart a little that I missed their maiden flight. But only a little.

The Season of Singing

Summer ✤ Week 1

Everywhere, from sunup to sunup, the world is full of song. The days are hot, hot, and all the hot day long I listen to the bees lifting from flower to flower, to the watchful chipmunk sounding its *chock chock chock* alarm while the red-tailed hawk wheels, crying, high in the sky. I can't see the songbirds in the dappled light of a thousand leafy branches, but I can hear them calling from the trees.

I watch the robins cock their heads at the sound of the earthworm moving within the soil. So much music I can't even hear!

A thunderstorm rolls in, and I open the door. I pull my chair right to the jamb and make of my house an anteroom, a portal straddling two worlds. In the heavy air I think of my father, hearing the boom of the thunder he loved, the hiss of the rain that cools the baked streets. Above the hot pavement, rain condenses into vapor.

Wind in the grass is a whisper. Wind in a pine tree is a hushing schoolteacher, her finger to her lips. At the back of the yard, wind in the broken black locust is a hungry howl.

Now the rain makes way for the undulating call of cicadas at sunset, its rising and falling, the pulse of the world. The cicadas' song overlaps the lighter, steadier call of the katydids and the percussive scritch of the crickets. *Summer, summer, summer*, they sing into the damp night. *Summer, summer, summer, summer.*

Praise Song for
the Skink Who Has
Gone to Ground

On YouTube there's a video of a man pointing at a big rock. When he stoops to upend the heavy stone, his companion's camera reveals an underground hollow where a broadhead skink is guarding her eggs. She is curled around them protectively. She does not stir when her secret is revealed. She will stay there until those eggs hatch.

The man shows us the skink and her eggs and then slowly sets the rock back down. He is taking care, but every time I watch this video I am worried for the far-more-careful mother skink. After the man puts the rock back in place, I want him to tell us that the skink is safe, that he has not crushed her in teaching us what a fine mother she is. I want proof *the skink is safe.*

But proof would require him to heave the rock up again, and more than I want to be assured that the skink is whole, her eggs unharmed, I want the man on YouTube to go away.

CLASS ... A; ORDER I. ANURA.   40?

... or less rapid ... the greater the heat the more speedy is the
... rates the progress of the young animal.

AND PROGRESS OF THE YOUNG FROG.

Fi... 1 presents the embryo ... appears several days after the e...
... g... line of it... f... wh...
... rin...

... d worms. This,
... e spec... of the family.

Thirty-Four Is Tadpoles

Summer ❧ Week 2

My stock-tank pond was coming along. While I waited for the aquatic plants I'd ordered to arrive, I filled in where I could. At the farmer's market, I found two nice pots of blue flag iris, native flowers that frequently grow at the edges of ponds. Blue flags are already among the early bloomers in my pollinator garden, beloved of newly emerged bees, but these two I "planted," pots and all, right inside the pond to mimic the way they occur in marshy places. Marginal plants provide crucial habitat for aquatic wildlife, including amphibians like the tree frogs I was hoping to attract. But two months after my youngest son and I spent an entire day setting up the pond, it was still bereft of frogs.

I've never understood why we have no frogs in our yard. On rainy nights I can hear Cope's gray tree frogs singing all over the neighborhood, including in yards that I know are treated with pesticides. Amphibians are indicator species, extremely sensitive to changes in the environment, vulnerable to toxic disruptions. So why did the tree frogs prefer the poisoned yards of my neighbors to our natural yard? A yard that now boasted a nursery pond built especially for them?

"Maybe it's because of your snakes," a naturalist friend suggested.

I hadn't thought of that. It's true that we have snakes in our yard. And it's true that many other predators in a wildlife-friendly yard make a habit of eating amphibians. In a choice between an invisible pesticide and a very visible garter snake, perhaps the frogs were taking their chances with Roundup.

Maybe, too, a pond made of recycled plastic just isn't attractive to frogs. Maybe it offers too few hiding places. For raccoons or crows, catching frogs in a bucket is literally like shooting fish in a barrel—they simply reach in and help themselves. Snakes can go hunting right *in* the water. While the islands of blue flags would be excellent places for frog morphs to rest and look around, potted plants are woefully inadequate cover from predators.

Plants that float in and on the water, on the other hand, can protect frogs and tadpoles and simultaneously help to keep the water healthy, adding oxygen and controlling algae. I really, really needed those plants I'd ordered, anacharis and hornwort and duck-weed, to fill the pond with dense greenery and make it safer for my amphibian neighbors. The more I thought about it, the more I realized I probably needed a few more marginal plants, too, to layer around the sides of the tank, for the same reasons.

So back to the farmer's market I went, coming home this time with inland sea oats and creeping Jenny and cardinal flower. A friend donated some horsetail, which grows quickly and spreads on its own, to plant in back. My stock-tank pond was starting to look less like a big bucket and more like an actual habitat.

But still no sign of a frog. Of the aquatic plants I'd ordered, perhaps not coincidentally, there was also still no sign.

. . .

"WHAT CAN I DO TO HELP?" Haywood asked one day while I was struggling to meet a newspaper deadline in time to pack for our anniversary getaway to the Cumberland Plateau. He was eager to get on the road before afternoon traffic picked up, but I was the only one who could meet that deadline. I was also the only one who knew what needed to go in my suitcase. The packing would be easy. The writing, as always, was a total crapshoot. I had no idea how long it would take me to finish that essay because I never know how long it will take me to write anything. The only way Haywood could help was not to hover.

Then it hit me: with school out for summer, here was a teacher with plenty of time to solve the problem of my missing plants. "Honey, would you call that pond-supply store and ask why they still haven't sent the plants I ordered two months ago?"

And that's how I learned that ordering online isn't the same thing as ordering from an online vendor: the pond store had received my order, yes, but all this time the staff had been waiting for me to drive out and pick it up. Haywood volunteered to go.

He came back holding a plastic bag full of stringy green plants and grinning. "I found the perfect present for you," he said.

I didn't understand. We don't generally give each other presents on our anniversary. "The plants?"

"I'll tell you tomorrow. On our anniversary," he said.

THE PERFECT thirty-fourth anniversary present, it turns out, is tadpoles.

In the outdoor tanks at the pond-supply store, Haywood had noticed some wild tadpoles wiggling among the aquatic plants.

When he mentioned to the woman at the cash register that we had failed to attract egg-laying frogs to our own container pond, she offered to catch a few of their tadpoles to donate to the cause.

"What kind of tadpoles?" Haywood asked.

Some of the tadpoles were huge, thumb-sized. "Maybe bull-frogs?" the clerk said. On the other hand, she'd nearly stepped on a tree frog a couple of weeks earlier, so possibly they were tree frogs. One of those two species. Possibly.

It worried me, this business of importing tadpoles from an unknown species into an ecosystem I was obliged to protect. On the other hand, leaving those tadpoles at the store, which was surrounded by a gravel parking lot that butts up against a highway, might be consigning the vast majority of them to their doom. I couldn't imagine how tadpoles had gotten into those display tanks in the first place.

The appearance of frogs where frogs have never been before is nearly always a mystery to me. There are two swimming pools in our neighborhood that were abandoned during the pandemic—one because the house burned down, the other because the owners of the pool had left town and couldn't get home again during the quarantine. Both swimming pools somehow filled up with frogs, many different kinds of frogs. All summer long they had made of the night a wild chorus of song.

"Frogs can travel quite a long way on a rainy night," my naturalist friend pointed out. But how? In this pondless neighborhood, hemmed on all sides by commuter surface roads, they traveled a long way from *where*?

The next week, after we returned from the Cumberland Plateau, Haywood and I went to pick up our tadpoles, whatever kind of tadpoles they might turn out to be. The clerk pulled out a plastic bag containing water, a cloud of algae, and three small tadpoles—way too small, I felt sure, to be incipient bullfrogs. That much was a relief, at least: I was not confident a forty-gallon stock tank could serve the needs of a single bullfrog, let alone three of them. I was even less confident that a bullfrog could find a bigger pond near enough to move to.

At home, we set the tadpoles free. They wiggled straight down, beneath the floating plants, and disappeared. That's when it occurred to me that this was destined to be the same old story of nature in medias res. I, with no idea where those tadpoles had come from, would also have no idea what happened to them next. Between the layers of vegetation and the layers of muck already gathered at the bottom of the bucket, I would never see them again.

A FEW DAYS LATER, I started to worry that we hadn't brought home sufficient algae to sustain the tadpoles until they were old enough to eat insects, so I read up on what people feed tadpoles in captivity. Then I went to the store and bought organic spinach. I was chopping up the boiled greens when Haywood wandered into the kitchen. "What's this?"

"Spinach. For the tadpoles."

He looked at me. I looked back at him.

"Got it," he said.

Twice a day I dropped a pinch of cooked spinach into my stock-tank pond, but I never saw a tadpole. I was faithful to the task, even leaving tadpole-feeding instructions for the house sitter when we went out of town for a long weekend, but I had no idea if those tadpoles were still alive. So much of what I do in this yard is only ever an exercise in hope.

. . .

YET MORE TIME PASSES, and there comes a day when I am standing next to the tank on a sunny afternoon, trying to persuade Rascal that he can pee right in the yard and does not need to take a walk in the blistering heat. For just a moment, the perfect slant of light emerges from behind a cloud bank to shine through the one patch of water that happens—also for just that moment—to be clear of floating plants. Briefly, the light brightens the mud at the bottom of the tank.

It would take a miracle for one of those tadpoles, if indeed any of the tadpoles are still alive, to scoot across that spot just when I am standing where I can see that bit of light reach that bit of mud.

But that's what happens. I am standing right there when a small black miracle propelled by a wiggling tail moves out of the darkness at the bottom of the tank and crosses the light. I am standing there still when it moves into the darkness again.

Praise Song for
the Red Fox, Screaming
in the Driveway

The red fox sits in my neighbor's driveway in plain view of the air conditioner repairman, who makes a video from the window of his van. Every time the fox opens his mouth, an unearthly scream erupts. Scream after scream after scream. If you heard this sound at night, never having heard a fox scream before, you would swear a woman was being murdered in the woods.

The fox is not interested in the repairman. He is screaming at a cat, who is also sitting in the driveway. My neighbor has a tender heart for animals. She knows the fox has a mate and kits in the woods behind her house, in uncomfortable proximity to her chicken coop, but she does not try to evict them. She reinforces the coop instead.

I hear the story of the fox screaming in my neighbor's driveway, and I think about the red-tailed hawk who once swooped down to get a better look at my baby in the grass. I think of the barred owl who did the same thing when Rascal was snuffling in the leaves. I think about the time someone walked into a bathroom at the downtown convention center and found a coyote sitting in the corner. Is it thrilling to know these predators are among us? Or is it heartbreaking to understand how thoroughly we have colonized their world? To know they have no choice but to make do with whatever vestiges of wildness we leave them?

Loving the Unloved Animals

Summer ✤ Week 3

Arise and drink your bliss, for every thing that lives is holy!

—WILLIAM BLAKE, *Visions of the Daughters of Albion*

S ing, O muse, of the lumbering opossum, of the nearsighted, stumbling opossum, whose only defenses are a hiss and a hideous scowl. Let us rejoice in the pink-nosed, pink-fingered opossum, her silvery pouch full of babies no bigger than a honeybee.

May the young opossums thrive to ride upon her back. May they fatten and grow large and stumble off on their own to devour cockroaches and carrion and venomous snakes. May their snuffling root the ticks from our yards and the snails from our flower beds. When they faint in the face of our baying hounds, let us guard them till they wake. Let us cheer when they rise and shake themselves. Let us send them off with our blessings as they blunder back into the night.

Let peals of gratitude ring out, too, for the glossy vulture, soarer of air currents, eater of gore. We gaze in wonder at the vultures' distant perfection, mistaking them for creatures we thoughtlessly love much more: eagles, hawks, ospreys. Slow in our heavy human bones, we follow them with our eyes, watching as they barely shift the angle of their wings to bank and glide, to circle and circle again.

Oh, vulture, may we remember in your circling the cycle you complete. On the ground, something is suffering. Something is coming near to the end of its time among us, but its life is not ending. Its life can never end. You are turning its body into something beautiful: blood and feathers and hollow bones. Earthbound no longer, the dead are rising again in you, rising and rising, lifted on air.

As the bright clarity of June gives way to hot July, let us consider the whine of the mosquito, the secrecy of the spider, the temper of the wasp—who among us could love you? Who could love even one of you, bearing your poisons and your pain into the thick, close air?

We could. We could love you if we reminded ourselves that no creature is made up only of poison, that no life is only a source of irritation or pain.

Let us love the mosquitoes for feeding the chittering chimney swifts wheeling in the sunset. Let us love the mosquitoes for feeding the tree swallows flying low over the lake at the park. We must love the spider for spinning the silk that holds together the moss of the hummingbird's nest, the silk that stretches as the baby birds grow. We must love the wasp for eating the caterpillars that eat the tomato plants. We could love you all if only we remembered the tree swallows and the hummingbirds, if only we remembered the taste of homegrown tomatoes still warm from the sun.

On endless summertime evenings, on cool and generous summertime evenings, let us speak kindly of the red bat, the homely little bat with the smushed face and the hairless infants clinging to her fur by teeth and thumbs and feet. In daylight, she dangles one-footed from a tree branch, masquerading as a dead leaf. At nightfall she unfolds her canny wings and skitters to her work in the sky, circling under the streetlights, clearing the air of moths whose larvae eat our trees, sweeping up all the biting, stinging creatures we swat at in the dark.

We behold the rat snake gliding through the nighttime weeds. We behold the sleek skin, cool but not damp, and the clever darting tongue, sniffing out the contours of the world. We watch as she finds the crack under the toolshed door, understanding that she is on her way to finding the baby mice tucked into a nest in the corner of a drawer full of rags.

Pity the young mice, born for just this purpose. Always there are mice—more mice than the world could hold if not for this beautiful, sinewy creature, this silent celebration of muscle and grace, this serpent serving our uses but too often coming to a brutal end at the end of a hoe.

World, world, forgive our ignorance and our foolish fears. Absolve us of our anger and our error. In your boundless gift for renewal, disregard our undeserving. For no reason but the hope that one day we will know the beauty of unloved things, accept our unuttered thanks.

Pickers

Summer ❧ Week 4

The crow stared at me and I stared back at him, and
looking into his eyes was like looking in a dark mirror.

—KATE DiCAMILLO, *Louisiana's Way Home*

Haywood and I have lived in this house for almost thirty years. Here we raised three children, buried five dogs, let an uncountable number of fallen leaves lie in a life shot through with leavings. All but a handful of our first neighbors are gone now. They have died in their own beds or gone off to die in beds that smell vaguely of bleach. No one will ever live in their houses again. One morning, after one of them leaves—for the retirement home, for the funeral home—I wake to the sound of a backhoe chewing down what's left of their lives here: the small rooms where their babies slept; the doorways where they stood when trick-or-treaters came at Halloween and carolers came at Christmastime; the windows where they waited, worried for a teenager who had not come home.

It is one thing to watch as plain, working-class homes are destroyed to make room for fine, fancy houses. It is another thing altogether for the unwavering shade trees and the raucous jumble of wildflowers to be mowed down, too, with no more thought than a lawnmower gives the grass. So much life cut off for no reason but commerce.

Even before a backhoe takes its first bite out of the perfectly sturdy roof that kept my old friends dry in storms, before the utility trenches kill any trees that survived the backhoe, the pickers arrive. They come for what is always called an estate sale, though the house is hardly more than a life-sized shoebox. I stop in sometimes, hoping to find a lasting memento of people whose lives overlapped with mine only circumstantially but for a long time. People who raise children together and look for lost dogs together and take time to visit in the street after supper can become friends, and their friendship is woven from many strands. Longtime neighbors can have more in common than colleagues, more than many siblings.

The last time I went to an estate sale, I bought an apron my friend wore when she baked, as well as a book signed by another neighbor whose death I still mourn. I tried on the apron and thought of the time my friend first mentioned her book club, the one she had joined as a lonely young mother. When I asked her which book they were currently reading, she laughed: "Oh, honey, we haven't read a book in fifty years."

On estate-sale days, cars line both sides of our narrow street. These are always expensive vehicles, polished trucks kept safely in a garage at night, late-model SUVs with cargo space to spare. They rarely belong to the people you'd think to find at yard sales, people with not enough money to buy something new. Mostly these are the well-off bargain hunters, the resellers with the cleverly arranged booths in antique malls on the edge of suburbia. They have come to pick the bones of the dead. I am hardly better, I know, me with my book and my apron, now 40 percent off.

Often the crows are quarreling in the treetops while the pickers load their cars. It's easy to think of them, too, as big jostling birds, ungainly carrion-eaters. But human beings are neither vultures nor crows. The world would count itself lucky if we were vultures or crows. An actual vulture turns death into feathers. An actual crow turns flesh into flight.

Of Berries and Death

Summer ❧ *Week 5*

The serviceberries came and went, and I didn't get so much as a taste—the mockingbirds plucked them from their stems as quickly as the berries could ripen. I've heard stories of determined old-timers who would keep close watch on woodland stands of serviceberry trees, sleeping beneath them to gather newly ripened berries at dawn, before the birds could lay claim. But feeding the birds is why I planted my serviceberries in the first place, and I am happy to cede every blue berry to them. I'm not certain I'd prevail in a contest with a mockingbird anyway.

The blackberry harvest is bountiful this year, enough for us and the mockingbirds, too. The thornless canes growing on the fence behind my pollinator beds aren't wild berries—they belong to a cultivated variety passed along by a friend—but the birds can't tell the difference, it seems, and I can't either. Any blackberry ripe in the summer sun, no matter the variety, is the taste of my childhood.

But there's a primitive connection in me that runs straight from blackberries to rattlesnakes. So many creatures feast on ripe blackberries that it's hard to imagine a more promising spot for a rattlesnake to set up camp, and every year when my canes are thick with fruit, when they are entwined with passion vines thick with blooms, I must work to remember that no rattlesnakes—shy creatures who would not be at home in this artificial neighborhood—are coiled beneath their tangles. "There are no rattlesnakes here," I repeat to myself. "I don't need to look for rattlesnakes." Though I am a profound respecter of snakes, I confess I am not sorry about the absence of rattlesnakes from this particular spot in the first-ring suburbs.

It's dumbfounding to me when I think about it now, the way our grandmother would send us—my siblings and cousins and me—out to pick blackberries, promising to make us a cobbler if we filled our pail. "Watch out for rattlesnakes," Mimi would say, with no more solemnity than if she were warning us to come home in time for supper. And that's how I know that rattlesnakes were common in that time and in that place, though they are imperiled today—by habitat destruction, by climate change, always by human ignorance. Anybody picking wild blackberries in the Lower Alabama of my childhood was almost certainly sharing that skein of canes with a hidden rattlesnake.

But thinking about Mimi's admonition, the careless way she handed us a pail and told us to keep an eye out, almost offhandedly, is also how I know that rattlesnakes take care to avoid human beings. My grandmother would not have sent us into danger. As long as we were careful not to step on a waiting snake, we were perfectly safe picking blackberries—as safe as any child can be in the fields or the woods, at least. In those days, no one would have thought to keep a wondering child away from the fields or the woods.

Here in this rattlesnake-barren yard in Tennessee, the pokeberries begin to ripen just as the blackberries are giving out. I sit at my writing table in our family room, the one in front of a row of windows facing a row of pollinator beds, and watch a brown thrasher and a mockingbird try to drive each other away, intent on protecting the pokeberries for themselves. I'm amazed when the thrasher wins the battle.

No one would camp out beneath a stand of pokeweed to beat the mockingbirds to the berries. Pokeweed is toxic to humans and dogs. The old poke salat of country lore, frequently mispronounced in pop culture representations of poor folk, is not a salad but a mess of cooked greens, and only the newest shoots of spring can be safely cooked. I am not a forager, and I have never tried to make poke salat—habitat is in such steep decline that I prefer to leave wild foods for wild creatures. Also, I don't trust myself. When a plant is edible only under certain conditions and poisonous under all others, I have no interest in testing my luck.

Haywood is so worried that the toddler next door might be tempted to help herself to a pokeberry that he has cut down the branch that hangs over the fence between our driveways, and I am careful to keep Rascal away from the berries that hang on our side. We needn't worry: the birds won't leave those berries alone long enough for even one of them to fall to the ground.

The Teeming Season

Summer ❧ Week 6

Now is the night one blue dew.

—JAMES AGEE, "Knoxville: Summer, 1915"

The world swells with fecundity, thick days and thicker nights pooling with song: cicada and tree frog and cricket and a thousand others I can't name. In the corners of our windows, spiders profit in the damp.

The fierce hummingbirds, who come to my feeders only every now and then in early summer, are back in earnest by late July, waging battles among the zinnias and the coneflowers and the bee balm to protect this territory. All day long, the bumblebees sink into blossoms, an embrace that looks so much like ecstasy it sometimes feels indecent to watch.

My favorite summer song is the cry of fledglings hollering for help from tree branches and the thickest shrubs, and sometimes in plain view from a fence post or a mailbox. They seem to be wholly unaware of the dangers they might be attracting. When he was little, I told my middle son that a mockingbird fledgling was calling to its mama, "Feed me! Feed me!"

"To a cat I fink it sounds like 'Eat me! Eat me!'" he said.

I love to hear the young jays screaming for a meal, as demanding as human teenagers perfectly capable of making their own sandwiches but hoping a sandwich will miraculously appear even so. "Is there anything in this house to eat?" my sons would ask, standing in front of a well-stocked refrigerator. If I pointed out all the options, they would clarify: "Is there anything in this house to eat that's already cooked?"

I laugh at the ungainly young crows, not yet so sleek as their parents, bumbling along on the ground, croaking like frogs and stumbling like drunks. I once saw a fledgling crow flip upside down while trying to balance on a power line. It dangled there for a moment, perhaps considering a poor flyer's limited options: let go and hit the ground, or flap and hang on, hoping to right itself. This youngster chose the former but lifted off again immediately after its graceless landing. Feathers can apparently do more than lift a bird into the air. They can also break its fall.

In July, there's hardly a reason to feed the birds in this yard that is well stocked with bugs and seeds, but I sometimes feed them even so, just to see them up close, their colors as bright as any summer flower. The red wasps, too, have babies to feed and help themselves when I set out mealworms for the bluebirds. I used to shoo them away—bluebirds respect the dagger of a red wasp as much as I do and won't come near any feeder a wasp has claimed—but I don't do that anymore. The world is fertile. In this yard, for now, there's enough to go around.

Praise Song for
the Carpenter Bees Eating
Our Fence to Ruin

Maypops hang from the passion vines twined among the blackberry canes, though it's too early yet for anyone in the yard to hazard a taste. Even the squirrels, who all summer long have been biting into the hard green pears at the back of our lot, impatient for the ripening, leave the green maypops alone. I am heartened to see them heavy on the vines, for there are years when we have no passion fruit, or only one or two.

This bumper crop is a sign that our carpenter bees are thriving: of all the pollinators, only a carpenter bee is large enough to pollinate a passionflower. The bees nest in the wood of the same fence posts that support the blackberry canes and the passion vines, so the bees are handy for the blooming. They are so intent on their work that sometimes they cling to a flower and sleep there, upside down, all night.

When the maypops ripen, they will fall to the ground to be picked apart by many hungry creatures—squirrels but also raccoons, even foxes and skunks. Until then, the flowers are feeding the bees, and the carpenter bees are serving the flowers. And when the fence, which we did not build and do not love, finally falls to ruin, the vines will spread out to make of the ground a bower and a banquet. A home.

Kept Safe in the Womb
of the World

Summer ❧ Week 7

> Once my eyes are closer to the ground, I see tiny fruiting
> bodies everywhere, a colorful regatta on a sea of decaying
> leaves and twigs.
>
> —DAVID GEORGE HASKELL, *The Forest Unseen*

I 'd finished writing, I thought, when I sent the essay to my editor,
but my editor had other ideas. Questions came back for which I
had no answers. Suggestions came back with which I did not
agree. The clock was ticking, I knew, and in New York the clock
ticks faster than it ticks here in Tennessee. I went to the woods
anyway.

People often ask how long it takes me to write an essay, and I
wish I knew how to answer. When I start, I don't know where I'm
going, and I don't know what wandering route I must take to get
there. The whole thing is an exercise in faith. It begins with an
image, a feeling, a vague sense of why something matters to me. It
never begins with a plan. I just start writing and trust the words to
keep coming. I need the words themselves to guide me, to tell me
where to go and why. When I lead workshops, I tell young writers

to write. That is my whole pedagogy: Just write. Trust the words to come. If they don't come, go for a walk.

Always I find more answers in a forest than I find in my own hot attic of a mind. Scientists have made studies of the walking brain, and the results are dumbfounding. Given a test that measures creativity, college students sitting at a table produced unremarkable results. But when scientists put them on a treadmill, or sent them for a walk around campus, their brains lit up like the night sky. The students who walked produced 60 percent more original ideas than the students who were seated.

The study measured only the cognitive effects of a body in motion, walking on a treadmill or along a familiar route. I would like to see an fMRI image of a mind in a forest, even one as carefully managed as my local park, where the trails are mulched with donated Christmas trees. A forest so small that the cars on nearby roads are audible from every place on the trail.

It was raining the day I was on deadline, and I like the woods best in rain. There are fewer people on the path. The dampness softens the ground and muffles the sound of my own footsteps. The heat-dulled leaves of the canopy grow visibly greener. The understory goes greener still.

Best of all, in a wet world deadfall and soil erupt into fungi. Delicate whorls of polypores make a bouquet of fallen pines. Bright elf cups are scattered across the leaf litter as though a parade has passed by. Glowing angel wing mushrooms fruit on the hemlock like a bridal veil trailing along the path. Chicken of the woods make yellow and orange ruffles fit for a square dancer's skirt. Oh, their marvelous fungi names! Firerug inkcap, turkey tail, witch's hat, stinkhorn, jelly fungus, shaggy scarlet cup!

These are flowers of the shady forest, the silent scavengers of deadwood and rotting leaves. In living trees, they can form a symbiosis, colonizing roots and helping trees absorb nutrients, creating vast underground networks that allow trees to communicate with one another and even share resources. In dead trees, fungi soften wood, making it hospitable for insects, a place that can be carved out by birds in need of a nesting site, or animals in need of a hiding place or shelter from the cold. Fungi, too, can turn death into life.

I rely on apps and field guides to identify mushrooms, but their color variations seem to be endless, and I have no idea if I'm right. I would never eat a mushroom that grows wild in the woods. There are too many ways to be dead wrong, an adjective I choose deliberately, and too many purposes for fungi when they remain in the woods. I squat, I admire, I take pictures, I move on.

In one fallen tree, the transformation has been unfolding for so long that a little cave has opened up where a branch once joined the living oak. Over years, dead leaves collected in the cavity and turned into soil. In the shelter of that death-opened place, new green life has sprung up: moss and clover and some sort of trailing vine I can't identify. In the center, as carefully arranged as if a florist had planned it for a centerpiece, rises one woodland violet. Every time I see it, I remind myself to come back in springtime to see it in bloom.

By the time I reached the violet that day, I had already stayed out too long, but suddenly I understood how to fix the problem in my essay. I texted my editor to tell him I was on my way back to my desk. As an apology for my tardiness, I included a photo of the secret terrarium in the fallen oak.

"Like a little tree womb," he wrote back.

And that's exactly what it is. It's what all trees are when we leave them alone.

System of ASTRONOMY, Tab. VI.

Ptolemaic

Fig. 92

our SYS

94

 action of y Superior Planets
S P O T O N M
Heaven

Solar SYSTEM

Fig. 93

STARS Fig. 91

Reverse Nesting

Summer ❧ Week 8

Time is but the stream I go a-fishing in. I drink at it; but
while I drink I see the sandy bottom and detect how
shallow it is.

—Henry David Thoreau, *Walden*

In the end, the house where Haywood and I raised our children
emptied not gradually but all at once. The oldest was long since
grown, and even the younger two had been gone before, of course,
off on travel-study programs, away at college for months at a time.
But for two pandemic years they were at home more thoroughly
than at any time since they had learned to drive. On their
work-from-home days, I could hear them on the other side of the
house, talking to colleagues on Zoom.

I was still teaching when my firstborn was small, so he went to
his own "big-boy school." By the time his younger brothers came
along, I was working full-time as a writer, and it was more eco-
nomical to have a babysitter come to our house. While I worked in
my home office, they played with the sitter in another room.
Having them home again decades later brought those sweet early
days back to me with an ache.

Well, this is how it's meant to go, I remind myself. In nature offspring don't dawdle and dawdle. Certainly they don't dawdle because they are worried about their old mama, working alone in an empty house all the day long.

ARE THIS YEAR'S BLUEBIRDS aware that only two of their first five fledglings survived? I don't know, but they have built a new nest now, and for me the delight of summer has been those surviving fledglings—one male and one female—from the first clutch. Their breasts remain speckled with the spots of babyhood, and they are still begging their father for worms, but they are also pitching in with their young siblings.

The fledglings will follow their parents to the mealworm feeder, perching on the edge of the bowl and gaping. The older birds ignore them, picking up worms and flying to the nest box a few yards away. The fledglings eventually seize worms, too, and follow, fluttering a bit before figuring out how to land sideways, on the wall of the box. Startled, I've watched from the storm door as they, too, take a turn poking their heads into the box to stuff a worm into an open yellow mouth. I had heard of first-clutch babies helping to feed second-clutch babies, but I'd never seen it happen before.

Bluebirds aren't community feeders like cedar waxwings, who remain in flocks even during the nesting season, a time when most flocking birds separate. Waxwings sometimes share resources, passing berries one by one, in a kind of avian bucket line, to birds who cannot reach the food themselves. Bluebirds are also not like crows, those intensely social birds who stay together in families for years and cooperate to drive away predators. There is some biological imperative operating with these fledglings that can't be explained by normal flocking behavior.

I suspect it's because the hot weather came very late this year, but when it came, it came with a vengeance. When these parents built their first nest, the damp days of spring lingered in the sixties and seventies, a temperature that prolongs the incubation period for eggs. By the time the female laid her second clutch, we were in the midst of a record-breaking run of brutally hot days—ninety-six, ninety-seven, one hundred, with heat indexes ten or twelve degrees above that. The female took to perching in the doorway of the nest box, perhaps to keep cool, perhaps to watch her mate feeding their fledglings.

In the heat of high summer, the second set of eggs hatched in record time, which meant that the fledglings had not yet dispersed to find their own territories. Emulating their father as they learned to hunt, maybe they had also learned to emulate feeding behavior.

This is only my theory. It's possible the fledglings simply looked into the nest box, curious about what their parents were doing, and saw the giant yellow target that is the open mouth of a nestling. The compulsion to shove something into such a mouth appears to be inborn in songbirds—online there's a video of a male cardinal, in the midst of his late-summer molt, standing on the edge of a backyard pond and faithfully dropping worms into the mouths of goldfish. "That's not a mouth you can ignore," a friend said when I showed her my photo of a gaping bluebird. "Nature wants that mouth stuffed full of worms."

Whatever is motivating the fledglings' behavior, it's biological, not emotional, but something about this family tableau, spread out before me on these hot summer days, is making me feel better.

WHEN OUR YOUNGER SONS moved to the other side of town, they took so much of our furniture with them that there was a visible hole in nearly every room of the house they left behind, the house they each came home to when they were two days old. After they left, I walked through the rooms and thought about how much the house looked like the scene of a crime. Burglars broke in, tore everything apart, and took all our valuables with them. Burglars broke into my house and stole my babies.

They were such nice babies.

When I was building my own nest, I wanted every room to be a sign of welcome. Picture books on the coffee table, a rocking chair next to the sofa, brightly colored placemats on the table—all long before my firstborn had even arrived. For his aquarium-themed nursery, I made two dozen paper-mache fish to hang from the ceiling and invited each of our friends and family members to paint one. "Granddaddy made this fish because he loves you," I imagined telling him. "Wibby made this fish because she loves you."

The fish frightened him once he became a toddler. "Dat fish wooking mean at me," he would tell us, coming into our room after bedtime. Haywood took down one offending fish after another, night after night, until finally there were no fish left hanging from the hooks that dotted the ceiling. But two years later, when we told our little boy that he would be a big brother soon, and that the baby would sleep in his room, he asked us to hang up the fish again so everything would be ready for the baby. His bravery gave me a new idea for what to say: "These fish are here because your brother loves you," I would tell the baby.

By the time another little brother was on the way, our oldest had big plans for the room that would be the nursery. He chose a blue-and-yellow celestial motif, with paper-mache wall hangings in the shape of a sun, a moon, and three stars—one for Dad, one for Mom, and one for each child. For the ceiling, he wanted to stick up whole constellations of glow-in-the-dark stars. Years later, once that baby became a teenager, he swapped out the wall hangings for hip-hop posters and sports-team banners, but he never took down the stars.

Now THIS HOUSE IS quieter than it has ever been, and I am nesting in reverse: giving away clothes my sons have outgrown, repurposing abandoned bedrooms, cleaning out closets to make space for items that have always been stored, by default, in the attic. Haywood and I are old enough now that we should really think twice before climbing the ladder into that attic.

The tiniest bedroom is now Haywood's study. In the past, he has always done his work in the classroom, staying at school as long as it took him to come home free and clear, all ours for the evening. He formed this habit when our first child was born, but he is near retirement now, and soon he will need a quiet place of his own for reading and writing. He had his pick of empty bedrooms. He chose the smallest because it looks onto the bluebird's nest box in the front yard.

Standing at the storm door, I watch the fledglings feeding the babies in the sunny box. There are many ways to be a family, I know, and some of them can take the form of a wonderful surprise. My children are grown, and I am ready for whatever comes next. But when the painters arrive to remove the dents and scratches and scuff marks of the growing-up years, I ask them to be careful not to paint over the growth chart marked on the kitchen doorframe. "And please don't take down the stars in the little bedroom," I say. "I want to keep the stars."

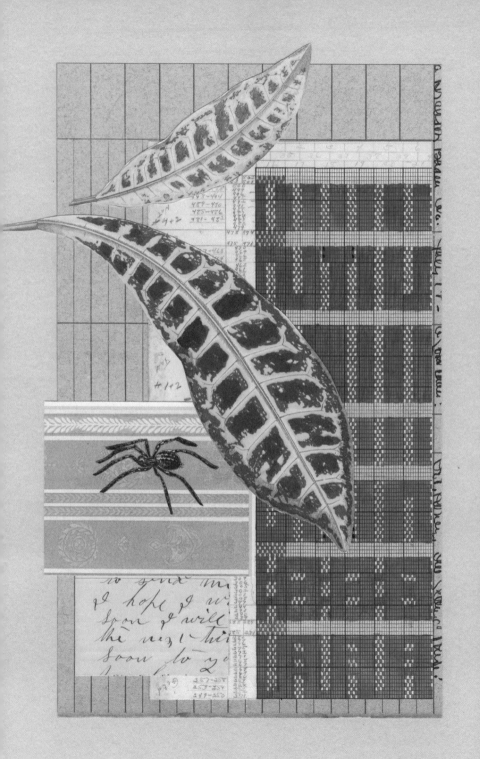

The Spider in My Life

Summer ꙮ Week 9

> Her six-inch mess of a web works, works somehow, works
> miraculously, to keep her alive and me amazed.
>
> —ANNIE DILLARD, *Holy the Firm*

A gray spider has set up an elaborate web at my writing table in the family room. She is not an orb weaver like E. B. White's famous Charlotte. This spider's web is a multilayered hammock-like construction strung between the leaves of the orchid I got for Mother's Day and anchored by silken strands to the window frame in back and to an African violet and a desk lamp on either side. I don't like to disturb my new deskmate, so I don't often water the plants. The orchid, a pink and purple confection with wide, glossy-green leaves, needs hardly any water. It is perfectly suited for this task. The violet has seen better days.

The spider's web is decorated with insect carcasses—three houseflies, countless fruit flies, and one desiccated former spider. A better housekeeper might be distressed about sharing space with a spider, but I love her. *Breaking news* is a term that has no meaning anymore—it's all as broken as broken ever gets—but the spider in my family room goes about her bloody business in the perfect order of things, unaware of the chaos unfolding beyond the window. An insect blunders into her web, and she eats it. Then she repairs the web and waits.

In times of fear and grief, it is tempting to assign human meaning to natural systems. How many people have told me that a loved one has returned to reassure them in the form of a mockingbird singing at midnight outside a silent house or a swallowtail butterfly lighting on a freshly carved tombstone? When the world has lost its still center, we grasp for any reminder that it is nevertheless spinning exactly as it must.

But my spider, for of course she is my spider now—one of those anchor lines has attached itself to my heart—is more than a symbol of the enduring natural order. She is more, even, than merely herself, performing the same motions her kind have performed for hundreds of millions of years. She is also the linchpin of a flourishing miniature ecosystem.

A few feet away from the spider's orchid bower, at the end of my writing table, sits a worm composter. It is populated by several thousand red wigglers who eat up our garbage. Every few days, I open the top of the composter and dump in a bunch of coffee grounds, banana peels, and vegetable parings, plus some shredded newspapers and junk mail, and the worms go to work making compost. When it's ready several weeks later, I take the compost outside and spread it in the pollinator garden.

In winter, when the insects are sleeping beneath fallen leaves and in the hollow stems of last year's flowers, the worm composter is a simple contraption populated almost exclusively by earthworms, but in summer other creatures find their way into it through open windows and doors, and they settle in. Whenever I lift the top of the composter in summertime, a cloud of fruit flies rises into the air.

Beyond the window where the spider has set up shop, there are two hummingbird feeders: one is the usual kind, filled with sugar water; the other is a newfangled contraption filled with rotting fruit. Fruit flies lay their eggs on the fruit. When the eggs hatch and the new flies exit through slits in the feeder, the ruby-throated hummingbirds in my yard catch them and feed them to their babies.

The process works fine with ordinary overripe bananas, but it works faster with pre-primed fruit from the composter. And thus do many of the fruit flies that begin their life in my family room make it to Central America transformed into a young humming-bird's feathers and bones. Meanwhile, any fruit flies that escape in the transfer from worm composter to hummingbird feeder are dispatched before they reach my kitchen by the spider on my worktable.

This kind of circular structure is what I love best about nature, even in its most violent reality. Outdoors, my spider's web might have been destroyed by hummingbirds, who build their nests partly of spider silk, and the spider herself might have been fed to the baby hummingbirds. Everything goes to some crucial use; nothing goes to waste. It makes sense. And things that make sense are particularly reassuring when the human world has turned itself upside down.

There is only so much information a person can take in during an emergency. There is only so much active resistance a person can engage in without succumbing to despair. Sometimes a body needs to rest. I have friends who pray more now, friends who drink more now, friends who read more novels or watch more television, friends who have taken up yoga or needlework or gardening. I have friends who wanted to adopt a kitten and then found that so many people had the same idea they had to get on a waiting list. A waiting list for rescue kittens!

I have tried some of these distractions myself, but I am taking my greatest comfort in a plastic bin full of earthworms turning garbage into food for flowers, in one spider crouching among a hundred silken strands that gleam like silver in the sunlight, in a cloud of fruit flies on their way to becoming a baby hummingbird's wings.

Praise Song for
What Hides in Plain Sight

If you're the tidy type looking at the scruffy base of this sugar maple, you see an unkempt yard, a weed patch. If you're an environmentalist, you see an unexpected pocket of biodiversity in place of the typical suburban monoculture. If you're my children, you see the tree where the rope swing once hung. If you're a dog, you see a good spot to pee. If you're a mama cottontail, you see the place where you hid your babies.

The dog on his leash cannot uncover this nest. The rat snake who ate all the chickadee nestlings has not found it in his rounds. Neither the cat two doors down nor the cat across the street has any idea it's here. I discovered the rabbit's secret only because this tree lies just beyond the mealworm feeder. When I stand at the storm door to watch the bluebirds, I can see the cottontail approach her nest at dusk.

She holds absolutely still while the babies nudge through the fur and grass she has tucked above them. She holds absolutely still while they reach for her, absolutely still for the few moments it takes them to feed. I can watch all this and never leave the house. Outdoors I give the tree a wide berth whenever I walk past. I am desperate to peek at the baby rabbits, but I don't want the rat snake to follow the scent of my footsteps in the grass.

My Life in Rabbits

Summer ❧ *Week 10*

Rabbits are everywhere among us.

—SUSAN ORLEAN, *On Animals*

Anna's Rabbit (1975)

We have a white rabbit now. I don't understand why my friend is not allowed to keep her pet, but the rabbit has come to live in a hutch in our backyard. He is huge, far too large to be pulled from a magician's hat. He weighs even more than our dachshund, who is massively overweight. I had no idea that rabbits could grow so big. Maybe his unexpected heft is why the rabbit lives with us now.

One weekend, not long after the white rabbit comes to live in our backyard, we get home after dark from my grandparents' house in Lower Alabama. When my father turns into the driveway, the headlight beams sweep across the front yard. I lean forward to see better. "It snowed while we were gone?" I ask.

In the front seat, my parents turn to look at each other. That's not snow.

Alabama Wildlife Rescue (1981)

The baby cottontails I am caring for are smaller even than the baby squirrels I have already released as a wildlife rescue volunteer. The squirrels drank their formula from a doll-size bottle, but for the first few days the bunnies need an eyedropper to feed. Only a few days, though—I could swear these soft creatures grow visibly bigger in just the time I leave them for class. The night before the day I have set for their release, I come back to my room to find their box empty, and it takes some time to find them. That night, to be safe, I close the box. The next morning, all three are stretched out on the bottom of the box, dead.

Next to the Maple Tree (the Last Year a Dog Was Allowed in the Front Yard)

The mower, its blade set as high as possible to protect rabbits and turtles, snakes and skinks, sweeps aside the top layer of a rabbit's nest we have never noticed. The mower deposits the cut grass back on top, and we don't see. The dog sees. This dog is only curious, entranced with the blind creatures that stir and cry out when he noses them. He doesn't mean to harm the one on top, but it screams nonetheless, a piteous sound its mother, hidden some- where nearby, surely hears.

I pull the dog away. Squatting, I try to think of what might keep these baby rabbits safe. The hollering one is silent now, and I return it to what's left of its nest in the crook between the raised roots of the maple tree. Immediately it burrows down among its brothers and sisters and sets them all in motion, too, a squirming pile of soft fur and rooting mouths. The heat from their bodies rises into the hot air—more heat than seems possible in an already burning summer.

I cup the nest and reshape it with my hands. The fur the mother rabbit has pulled from her belly to set on top of her babies beneath the grass—that warm, sheltering layer—is now wafting across the yard in the breeze. I tug some longer blades of grass around them, gather some pine straw to add on top. All day long I keep the dog inside. All day long I fight the urge to push aside the straw and check on the babies.

When Haywood gets home, he pulls out some old fencing shoved behind the toolshed and fashions a barricade around the rabbit's nest. A few snips with a bolt cutter, and now there's a rabbit-sized hole, just big enough for the doe to get through but not big enough for the dog's shaggy head. I pull a chair onto the front stoop and wait at the rabbit hour. I hear the great horned owl. I hear the neighbor's dog, and another neighbor's answering dog. Not another creature stirs in the failing light.

I worry. Will she come back? Can she reach her babies if she does come back? What about the rabbit fur scattered across the yard—will it summon the kinds of predators that no jury-rigged fence can hold back? Will the makeshift nest provide enough protection if it rains?

The next day the dog finds something a few feet beyond the fence. He pushes it with his nose and waits. Pushes and waits. I walk over. It's a dead baby rabbit. I take it from him and tuck it into the brush pile, where some hungry thing will eat it.

Inside, I call wildlife rescue. From my own volunteer days, I know there's not much they can do over the phone, but I call anyway. I need to know if the rabbit kit crawled out of the nest to die. Did it die of internal injuries caused by the curious dog? Was it starving, scratching its way through the fence because its mother couldn't reach it?

The helpline volunteer tells me to wait till early morning, open the fence, reach past the pine straw, and pull out one of the kits. Check it quickly and put it back, she says. If its belly is full, there's nothing more to worry about.

That warm little belly is tight as a tick.

Praise Song for the First Red Leaf of the Black Gum Tree

The cicadas are singing all day long, and the woods are green, green—impossibly, ridiculously green, and still the green deepens with every hot storm, every breath of dampness the heavy clouds unload. The bluebirds are trying to make up their minds about starting again in the nest box where they have already raised two broods this summer, and the blue jays have not yet begun to lose their blue.

We have come to August, a time when summer has gone on for so long that winter is scarcely a memory. It's more like a movie we once watched but whose details we can no longer recall: the title is gone, the actors' names, even what the story was about. This is the time of summer when summer tells us it will never end.

But here is an ancient black gum rising so high I'm obliged to throw my head all the way back to see even its lowest branches, and next to its trunk is a single red leaf, fallen onto the porous forest floor. A leaf so red it becomes the paradigm of redness, gathering into itself the red of the hummingbird's throat, the red of the redbird's crest, the red of the broadhead skink's courtship finery, the red of cardinal flowers nodding beside the stock-tank pond. It has taken into itself every gorgeous red that summer can offer and transformed it into something new.

I can hardly believe what it is telling me, dripping in the cloud-drenched woods, but I recognize it now: a prophesy.

Dislocation

Summer ❧ Week 11

Like them, I have sought to comfort and / so be
comforted.

—Vievee Francis, "Like Jesus to the Crows"

September, and the hardwood trees are still bright green.
Temperatures remain in the nineties, feeling nothing like fall,
but the chipmunks have already lost their minds. If I spill the bird-
seed, it's no time before they are up the spindles and onto the deck,
stuffing their cheeks to the point of comedy and then rushing back
to their burrows under the house, stocking up for winter.

Chipmunks are not cooperative creatures. Except during mating season, or to bark out warnings of a predator on the prowl, they
forsake the companionship of their own kind. Their unconnected
tunnels spread like arteries beneath the crawl space of our house,
but I rarely see them in summer. Now, with autumn coming on,
they are scooping up seeds like warm-blooded Roombas, ignoring
one another, maneuvering under my chair and between my feet as
if I weren't there.

The chipmunks are not alone in preparing for a changing season. Hot as it still is, the winter-flocking birds—starlings and

robins and blue jays and crows—are already beginning to gather again. All summer they kept to their individual tasks, building their nests and tending their young, but their fledglings are more or less self-sufficient now. After months of near silence in the shady woods, the crows are back to talking among themselves.

The last of the milky magnolia petals are going brown, and the bees are working the remaining pollen with all the focus of a lonely soul at a dive bar's last call. A few lightning bugs still wink beneath the trees at dusk, but the cicadas that have been singing in the branches all summer are beginning to weaken and lose their grip. I once saw a cardinal, her head nearly bald from her August molt, snatch a fallen cicada from the grass and carry it across three yards before disappearing with it behind a neighbor's house. I could hear the cicada crying out as it was borne away.

The fall before we married, Haywood and I went camping outside Berea, a college town in the Appalachians of central Kentucky. Poking around the town's art galleries, we found a potter who adorned the edges of her hand-thrown dishes with subtle reminders of the earth from which the clay had come—a four-petaled flower, a stalk of grass gone to seed. We fell in love with it. My mother had been after us to choose a tableware pattern for our still-nonexistent wedding registry, but these dishes were so much nicer than anything in a department store. Each plate, each bowl and mug was clearly part of a set and at the same time utterly unique. Irreplaceable. The potter agreed to take orders from our friends and family members, keeping track of who ordered what, and some months later our beautiful wedding dishes arrived.

When our first child was performing the usual gravitational studies of toddlerhood, tossing everything off the table, we learned the hard way that our irreplaceable plates needed to be put away till our son—and, later, his brothers—was old enough not to destroy them. It wasn't until our youngest sons were packing to move that I suddenly remembered our wedding dishes, still in the attic decades after we hauled them up there. We gave our sons the ordinary white plates they had grown up with and installed our wedding dishes in the kitchen cupboard. We eat on those plates every night now. Sometimes, in the quiet house, we remark on their loveliness and remember to each other how they came to be ours. We have not yet learned how to cook for only two.

Abundance is the story of approaching autumn, in our lives and in our yard. The southern arrowwood bushes are adorned with bright blue berries, and the branches of the sugar maples are thick with seeds. From a distance it looks as though the trees have turned brown long before it is time for them to go golden. Every limb, every twig is dense with seeds, a load so heavy that the lower branches are nearly brushing the ground. It's a mast year for maples, and I wonder if they somehow know how many other nearby trees have been felled this year and so are bearing seeds enough for them, too.

The drooping petals of the coneflowers are dry and brittle now, and the goldfinches are tearing apart the seed crowns, picking each seed from its spiky carapace. This is a garden for pollinators, so when I remember to, I deadhead the flowers to force the plants to keep producing blooms instead of seeds. I never deadhead the coneflowers, though, for there are few things more beautiful than the sight of a goldfinch still wearing his summer finery and riding a coneflower tossing in the autumn wind.

A new slant of light signals the changing season even in this humid heat. The ruby-throated hummingbirds know it and are bulking up for their long flight, guarding every nectar source before they go. The dominant bird, a young male, takes up his patrol from the pokeweed branches, where he has a clear view of the large pollinator patch in the front yard and the smaller patch next to the driveway. In this way he can swoop upon any encroachers and chase them entirely out of the yard.

Up at the cabin, where there are more hummingbirds and also more branches to perch on, the birds engage in a ceaseless aerial war that rises high into the trees, a chittering swirl observable from any window in the place. Soon they will all make their way south to their wintering grounds in Central America. Some will go by land. Others will fly directly across the Gulf of Mexico. In the meantime, they fight for dominance over the feeders. Adding more feeders does nothing to resolve their disputes. There is plenty of food to go around, plenty of insects and plenty of seeds, but wild creatures have no interest in sharing.

For us, too, change is almost always a source of dislocation, but if nature teaches us anything, it's that nothing prevents the passage of time, the turning of the seasons. It might be a long time coming, as Sam Cooke so gorgeously sang, but a change is gonna come. I take his words as a pledge.

Praise Song for
the Ragged Season

All the children are gone now, packed off to their own lives, and my husband, a teacher, has settled into the new school year. I am the only one here who is still a little bit lost and a little bit ragged.

I stand at the window looking out, trying to remember the truths that nature always brings home. That what lies before me is not all there is. That time is ever passing, and not only when I notice. That strife and pain are no more unexpected than pleasure and joy. That merely by breathing I belong to the eternal.

I watch the bald cardinals feeding their fledglings, and I know they feel awful. I remind myself of what I cannot remind them—that raggedness is just the first step toward a new season of flight.

Fig. 8.

The World Is a Collage

Summer ✤ Week 12

Earth teems with sights and textures, sounds and
vibrations, smells and tastes, electric and magnetic fields.
But every animal can only tap into a small fraction of
reality's fullness.

—ED YONG, *An Immense World*

S top!" I say, grabbing my husband's arm and pulling him back.
It is Rascal's last walk of the night, and we are taking a path
around the neighborhood that we have taken every night for years.
It is as familiar to us as the way through the dark house that leads
from our room to the rooms where our children slept. But now
something has flown out of the night and landed just where
Haywood's foot will fall with his next step. He stops. I open the
flashlight app on my phone.

On the street crouches an obscure bird grasshopper, a large
insect aptly named. Ask me how I know this, and I will tell you
about the time an obscure bird grasshopper flew into my pollinator
garden while I was weeding. I looked up expecting to see a wren.

I squat to look more closely. Grasshoppers cannot turn their
heads, but this one shuffles its whole body a quarter turn to look

back at me. "It's hard to believe there's anything wrong with your eyes," Haywood says for what is probably the thousandth time in our marriage. "You saw that bug in the dark!"

In fact there are many things wrong with my eyes. To see small creatures, I look for signs of disparity, or I follow some new sound or motion. If something isn't clearly distinct from its surroundings, or if it isn't singing or running or crawling or flying, I will almost certainly miss it.

I have limited depth perception, a consequence of uncorrected amblyopia in childhood. And lodged in the optic nerves of my eyes are structures called drusen, which, like amblyopia, are congenital— in time they may cost me my peripheral vision. Drusen likely caused my mother's macular degeneration and may have been the reason her brother lost his vision to ocular hemorrhages. My grandmother went blind from a hereditary form of glaucoma. The genetic legacy from my father's side of the family is more devastating—a very high risk of cancer—but I don't dwell on that possibility. It still feels distant to me, more theoretical than real. The family history of blindness, on the other hand, I think about more and more often as I leave midlife behind. The accruing indignities of a body that is no longer predictable makes it hard not to ponder what other burdens might lie ahead.

And now I have cataracts, too. This is a common problem for people in the last third of their lives, of course—a problem that's easily remedied, at least for the fully insured. It is nothing to panic about. I panic anyway, just a bit. The specialist who monitors my vision tells me that he can remove the cataracts before they get worse, before they begin to interact in a more troubling way with everything else that's wrong with my vision. Already a new blind spot has turned up on the elaborate testing I undergo every year, though it's still unnoticeable to me. Almost all the effects of cataracts have been invisible to me so far because I have grown accustomed to incremental change, to vision that is always a little worse from one year to the next. I order new glasses, spend a few days getting used to the updated prescription, and then stop thinking about it. I see what I can see. I have no way of knowing what I cannot see.

The world is becoming dimmer to me whether I am aware of it or not. Colors are fading. I can no longer remember a time when the streetlights did not have halos. The doctor entices me with promises of brighter colors and crisper lines. Good God, I think, how much more beautiful the beautiful world would be with even more color! Within hours of having her first cataract removed, my mother could not stop marveling over the flowers. They were her *own flowers*, but she had not yet seen them for what they really were.

I am afraid. I have lived with the fear of losing my sight since I first understood my family history, and there is a non-zero risk—as my sons like to call a very small chance—that this ordinary and safe operation will make my vision worse. How could I bear to see even less?

Even with perfect vision, a human being's ability to perceive the world through sense experience is limited. A red-tailed hawk can see a mouse in the grass from a hundred feet in the air. Raccoons have four times as many sense receptors in their hands as we do. To keep songbirds from crashing into our storm doors, I put up stickers impregnated with a chemical that reflects ultraviolet light, which birds can perceive but people cannot. I watch Rascal sniffing and sniffing at the same spot in the ditch at the edge of our yard, and I know that another dog has marked it. Rascal can tell if the dog who peed there was male or female, healthy or sick, calm or agitated. I can't tell another dog was ever there.

Animals have many, many ways of apprehending their world that I can imagine only poorly, if at all. The way the pupils of a Cooper's hawk dilate at the sight of prey. The way a robin migrates by tuning into the earth's magnetic field. The way rattlesnakes can find their prey by following infrared radiation. The way bats send sound waves into the dark, and the way what comes back to them is the shape of the world. I think of the marvelous compound eye of the housefly, creating a mosaic from thousands of images. For a housefly, the world is a work of collage art, patched together but whole and hopelessly, extravagantly beautiful.

Praise Song for
the Holes in Pawpaw Leaves

Pawpaw trees don't bear fruit for years. The saplings I've planted are a long way from feeding the opossums, foxes, squirrels, raccoons, and birds I planted them for, but even now their leaves could feed the caterpillars of the zebra swallowtail butterfly, just as the pokeweed leaves feed the caterpillars of the giant leopard moth long before the pokeberries are ripe enough to feed the birds. I have never seen a zebra swallowtail butterfly in this yard, or a giant leopard moth, either, but I know the leopard moths are here by the holes in the pokeweed leaves. If ever holes should appear in the pawpaw leaves, too, you will hear my shouts of delight and know the cause of my rejoicing.

Imagination

Summer ❧ *Week 13*

The remnants of the hurricane arrived days after we understood it was coming. Even a direct hit on the Gulf Coast means that the worst of the weather will take a while to get to us in Tennessee. We knew it was on the way, but we did not fully grasp what it would bring: ten inches of rain overnight, two tornadoes, outmatched rivers and creeks, roads submerged in the runoff. Rain was coming in through the tops of our closed bedroom windows, and Haywood and I spent a good part of the evening moving furniture, tying back curtains, and setting lasagna pans on ladders to catch the blasting water. Tornado sirens always make me wish our house had a basement, but even with the sirens going off for hours, I was glad we didn't have a basement to fill up with rain that night.

Out in the pollinator garden, the young ruby-throated hummingbird who had claimed our feeder kept steadfast watch over his personal nectar source. The rain was blowing horizontally, but he clung to his perch and simply shook off the raindrops from time to time, shivering and ruffling his tail feathers. Male ruby-throats don't have that telltale scarlet gorget until after their first molt, so I knew this territorial fellow was hardly more than a baby. He had never attempted the long migration himself, and no hummingbird lore had told him to fatten up for it. But the days were growing shorter, the slant of light changing, and so his body had signaled him to feed as often as he could. Any day he would start flying south.

I don't tend to anthropomorphize the creatures in my yard—partly because I find their alien ways so interesting, and partly because thinking of them in human terms only makes the constant tragedies feel more tragic—but it can be hard for me not to see them as metaphors. I watched that hummingbird hunched down in a cold rain, resolute and undefeated, preparing in his unconscious way for a journey whose dangers he couldn't predict, and I thought, "I should be more like that." Flexible, adaptable, untraumatized by change.

And then I thought, "Stop it. Nature is not a sermon."

What I imagine is happening in the minds of the creatures in my yard is merely that, an act of imagination. I am guessing. I am projecting from my own experience, an experience that is entirely unlike the hummingbird's experience.

Then I opened the newspaper to find a front-page story about the wildfires that had earlier engulfed East Tennessee. A federal review had identified a calamitous failure of imagination as a chief reason for the fire's deadly magnitude. "It was simply impossible for the park and first responders to imagine and react to this combination of conditions," said the wildfire expert who led the review.

That's when I understood: imagination isn't necessarily a wrong-headed way to encounter nature. I took my cup of coffee to the window, where a steady rain was still blowing. The little hummingbird sat unmoved at his perch.

Praise Song for
Fingers That Do Not Form a Fist

An insect, its name lost among those orders of creatures who number in the millions, has somehow found its way into the kitchen sink. This is not an indoor bug, not one of the ordinary housemates who dwell in the corners of the kitchen cabinets, beneath the unmade beds. How easy it would be to wash this bug out with the pasta water in the pot that has been soaking overnight, but please hold back. Surely the world harbors death enough already.

It's too easy to choose ease, too convenient to choose convenience, but try to take the harder path, for the harder path is not very hard. The creature scurries into the corner of the sink and tries to climb the slick walls. Reach toward it. When it climbs into your palm, gently close your fingers around it. Be careful to hold your thumb to the side. If you never close your thumb around your fingers, you will make of your hand a sanctuary. You will make of your hand safe passage to the world.

The Season of Making Ready

Fall ✤ Week 1

Fall is hurricane season, and whenever the Gulf Coast takes a wallop, the rains barreling north usher in a few blessedly cool days in the midst of our usual heat and haze. I wouldn't wish a hurricane on anyone, but I admit to feeling grateful for the rain. One September I drove home to Alabama while a gray mist turned the Appalachian foothills into a landscape of enchantment. Fog gathered in the valleys and edged the fields; shreds of clouds clung to the trees like a shroud. Solitude and silence made it easy to forget the existence of anything else. What is an automobile, what is an interstate, when all the world is folded into mist?

I have to work to love September, that in-between time when the heavy heat lingers but the maple leaves have already started to turn. Everyone is making ready—preparing in this time of plenty for the days of want ahead. In the garden, only the zinnias are still blooming, and even they are shabby and dusted with mildew. The gleaming crows cling to the power lines, panting.

The indefatigable bees and butterflies aren't troubled by the zinnias' curling leaves or the gray powder that coats them. Our resident hummingbirds are gone now, but weary migrants keep arriving to visit the fresh blooms. As much as hurricane rains in the Gulf can bring relief to us here in Tennessee, it's wrong to hope for rain while butterflies and hummingbirds are on the wing. For travelers, the journey is long. For residents, the preparation is hard. For all of us, winter is coming.

Praise Song for
a Clothesline in Drought

As I am shaking out the sheet, before I've even pinned it to the line and stepped away, the minutest winged creatures land on it to drink from the damp fibers. They are thirsty in this dry time, too small to drink safely from the birdbath or even the bee fountain. They drink the water from this sheet as though it were a leaf damp with dew, as though it were a rock slick with rainwater. Their fleet wings glint in the sun, bedazzling our bedclothes. Light upon light upon light.

Autumn Light

Fall ⚘ *Week 2*

I told him that I chose botany because I wanted to learn
about why asters and goldenrod look so beautiful together.

—ROBIN WALL KIMMERER, *Braiding Sweetgrass*

Autumn light is the loveliest light there is. Soft, forgiving, it
makes all the world a brightened dream. Dust motes catch
fire, drifting down from the trees and rising from the stirred soil,
floating over lawns and woodland paths and ordinary roofs and
parking lots. It's an unchoreographed aerial dance, a celebration of
what happens when light marries earth and sky. Autumn light
always makes me think of chalk dust settling in the expectant hush
of an elementary school classroom during story time, just before
the bell rings and sets the children free.

In fall, the nights are cooler and clearer, too, with the harvest
moon floating steadfast in the night sky. Along the roadsides, in
years when there's been enough rain, flowers bloom in wild bou-
quets: asters and ironweed and white snakeroot and goldenrod, as
high as my head—food for the monarchs and the painted ladies
and the ruby-throated hummingbirds as they make their long
migrations. Every kind of New World warbler is on the wing now,

heading south like the raptors and the waterbirds, but they linger a while before moving on again, and for a time Tennessee is filled with exotic songs.

The flowers that bloom in autumn, like the beautyberries and hackberries and arrowwood berries, don't deliberately signal the season of farewells. They are only blooming and ripening in their time, just as the birds and the butterflies are traveling in theirs, a perfect concatenation of abundance and need. But a lifetime of paying attention to what feeds my winged neighbors means I can't help seeing these dust motes, and these long shadows at the end of shortening days, as an irrefutable sign: summer is ending. By the time of the equinox, summer has already gone.

There was a time when I didn't feel sad about the coming of fall, perhaps because I grew up in Alabama, where the new season mostly means the end of unrelenting heat and oppressive humidity. There are plenty of warm, sunny days in an Alabama winter, and camellias bloom in profusion from November until the first blossoms of springtime arrive. That's not true here in Tennessee, where temperatures dip much lower at least once or twice each winter.

But perhaps the reason I didn't feel sad about the onset of fall when I was younger is only that I was younger, with my whole life still ahead. In those days my only worry was that my real life, the one I would choose for myself and live on my own terms, was taking too long to arrive. Now I understand that every day I'm given is as real as life will ever get. Now I understand that we are guaranteed nothing, that our days have always been running out.

And so I greet this season with a quiet and a stillness I never felt when I was younger. I used to laugh at the comical shabbiness of the bluebirds in molt, so fussy with one another as their new feathers come in. Now I know it won't be long before these fledglings, whom I have known since their mother laid the eggs they emerged from, will be off in their gorgeous adult blues to search for their own territories.

An orb weaver who pitched her camp next to my outdoor faucet this summer is making her egg sacs now. She, too, will be gone by the time cold weather arrives, but unlike the hummingbirds, she will not be coming back. Her future lies in the perfect egg sacs strung together like pearls and hanging in the center of her elaborate web—six of them now, with more to come, I think.

The gift of the equinox, the day when there are as many hours of light as of darkness, is the gift of Janus, of looking ahead even as we look behind. The summer birds are flying south and soon the broadhead skink will be looking for a safe place to spend the winter. I will watch for her to wake next spring, just as I will watch for the warblers and the hummingbirds to return, just as I will watch for this summer's seeds, carried on the winds of autumn and in the bellies of birds, to push up from the earth and bloom again.

And all winter I will keep watch over the spider's egg sacs, hoping that one of her daughters chooses this quiet spot for her own web. It's a good place to settle—damp and shady, a respite from the harsh light of summer.

Flower of Dreams

Fall ✤ *Week 3*

Virgie looked at the naked, luminous, complicated flower,
large and pale as a face on the dark porch. For a moment
she felt more afraid than she had coming to the door.

—Eudora Welty, "The Wanderers"

For decades, my grandmother was the caretaker of a gangly,
disorganized houseplant with nothing, so far as I could see, to
recommend it. The plant was ugly, an awkward tangle of greenery
fashioned from what seemed to be spare botanical parts: long
stems that reached out in a vaguely threatening way and generated
new stems, randomly, from within their own stretching expanses.
Some of the stems were round and some were flat and some were
almost serrated, and there were no leaves at all. It was less a plant
than something out of a nightmare. As a little girl, I thought it
might bite me.

In warm months, the plant stayed on the front porch of that
equally gangly, equally disorganized old farmhouse, a dogtrot
structure that had been added onto willy-nilly over the years.
When the evenings began to cool in early autumn, my grandmother would bring the plant indoors, set it on a table next to the

fireplace, and wait hopefully for it to bloom. She called it her
"night-blooming series."

It was years before I understood that the scary plant in my
grandparents' house was actually a night-blooming cereus, a catch-
all term for several varieties of cactus that bloom at night, often for
only one night each year. That's *if* they bloom: my grandmother's
"series" apparently bloomed just once in all the decades she had it.
There are two pictures of it in full flower, and they were both taken
on the same night sometime during the 1960s.

I have no idea how my grandmother, a teacher in a two-room
schoolhouse tucked among peanut fields in Lower Alabama, came
to be in possession of such an exotic plant, but I understand her
attachment to it, despite its annual failure to produce a bud. My
own night-blooming cereus has so far proved to be a non-blooming
cereus, too. All it grows are ridiculous appendages. One stem is
ninety-two inches long and still going.

This variety of cereus is a pass-along plant, easily shared via
rooted cuttings. My cutting came from my brother and sister-in-
law's plant, a proven bloomer, and I protect it ferociously. As much
as I welcome the obscure bird grasshopper that has taken up residence in our yard, I carefully removed it from the cereus, returned
it to the pollinator garden, and then zipped the entire plant into a
butterfly cage to protect it from future grasshopper incursions.

One year Billy texted a photo of a bud on his plant. "It might
bloom tonight!" he wrote. "I looked in my garden journal, and it
was fully open by 8:00 p.m. in 2014."

My brother's garden journal is a force of nature in its own right,
a combination of art and field notes that he adds to as time per-
mits and observations require. The years are layered one upon
another—notes from a specific date in one year sharing the same

space with notes from the same date a decade earlier—in an abundant approximation of the way the garden itself experiences time. Billy is a careful chronicler of his exquisite garden, and I had full faith in his best guess about the time his cereus would bloom.

I shot Haywood a text about where I was going, got in the car, and drove straight to Clarksville, more than fifty miles away. I stopped only for gas. With a night-blooming cereus, the transformation from bud to blossom can take less than an hour.

Driving west into the sunset, I squinted against the glare the whole way, but I could see well enough to note how dry the trees along the highway were—dry and covered with dust. The fall wildflowers had yet to appear. Believe me, I recognized the irony. There I was, driving through a climate-parched landscape with a full tank of gas, on a pilgrimage to do nothing more than watch a flower bloom. The hot winds from the eighteen-wheelers shook my whole car as they passed.

I am only one generation removed from the farm, and I spent much of my childhood in the world where my mother grew up: the same one where my grandmother grew up, and my great-grandmother before her, going back further than anyone can remember. For weeks of every year, I slept in the bed my mother slept in as a child; I walked barefoot down the same red-dirt roads she walked down barefoot; I ate the plums that grew beside her childhood porch, at least until they fermented in the hot Alabama sun and made the red wasps drunk on their wine.

Today only 2 percent of Americans live on farms or ranches, but we have not lost our need to be among green things. Which may explain my brother's impulse to keep a garden journal, and my own impulse to write about the life of my wild yard. It may explain why many friends and neighbors were already gathered in my brother and sister-in-law's living room by the time I got to Clarksville that evening, all of them waiting for the miraculous event to unfold.

The bud of a night-blooming cereus is a feat of botanical magic, big enough to span the full length of a human hand. This one was in no hurry to open. Pink filaments still ribbed it tightly from stem to tip an hour after I arrived. "It's like counting contractions, waiting for a baby to be born," someone said.

Then, finally, an aperture began to open at the very end. The pink filaments began to loosen and lift. As the aperture widened, a star-shaped structure unfolded within it—a white star inside a white flower—and the translucent petals unlayered and arrayed themselves around the star. The flower was nine inches across fully opened, and its perfume filled the whole room with sweetness.

It was not a nightmare plant. It was the flower of dreams.

It was just one flower on just one ordinary day in September. It would be gone by morning, not to return for another year. Its arrival did nothing to mitigate the drought gripping the land. It did nothing to feed a native pollinator or shelter a tree frog. You could insist that it didn't matter in any way, and I would not think to argue with you.

But it was also not nothing. That night-blooming cereus brought my grandmother back to me in her halo of white hair. It brought back, too, her plum tree, long since cut down, and the feeling of red dirt between my toes. For an hour, just this once, it made me remember what it feels like when the world is exactly as it must be, and I am exactly where I belong.

Praise Song for
the Back Side of the Sign

The sign says, "Keep Out."
The sign says, "Private Property."
But all along the road, the woods keep calling, Here! Come here!
Step off the pavement and come here, where the ground is soft and forgiving.

Come here, where the goldenrod is blooming in all its many guises and all its golden profusion—wreath goldenrod and Canada goldenrod and rough-stemmed goldenrod and dwarf goldenrod—wherever the sun finds its way to the place where a tree has fallen, or along the track that generations of deer have made with their delicate feet.

Step into the shade and come here, where the broad-winged hawk is teaching her young to hunt.

Here, where the chipmunk has folded its forefeet to its chest and reared up to call its warning chock chock chock *to all the other woodland creatures.*

Here, where the box turtle trundles into the stippled light of the underbrush, saying nothing.

None of them are talking to me, but I feel the murmuring as a welcome. It is a mother's hushing of a baby fighting sleep, a note slipped beneath desks when the teacher isn't looking, a call to prayer across the rooftops in a land I have only visited in books, the notes of a song drifting out of a room with the door propped open.

The Last Hummingbird

Fall ✤ Week 4

In fact, they are bubbles—hummingbirds are made of air.

—SY MONTGOMERY, *The Hummingbirds' Gift*

From inside the air-conditioned house, the light through my windows looks the way October light is supposed to look—mild, quiet, entirely unlike the thin light of winter or the sparkling light of spring or the unrelenting light of summer. In normal years, October is a month for open windows in Middle Tennessee. For cool, damp mornings. For colored leaves that quake in the wind before letting go and lifting away. For afternoon shadows so poignant they fill me with a longing I can't even name.

Relief is on the way, the forecast tells us, but the most we have had of autumn so far is the right slant of light, for this year the mild October light has not brought the usual mild temperatures. For all of September it was August in the South, and for early October, too—severe drought and temperatures near a hundred degrees, day after day after day.

My own yard is as drought tolerant as I can make it, planted with native trees and shrubs that evolved for this growing zone. Hardly a blade of water-craving grass is left here; self-seeding wildflowers have gradually crowded out the turfgrass over the years. But the wild ground cover crackles now when I walk on it, and little puffs of dust rise from the arid soil.

The once-fragrant piles of damp earth that moles turned up in the night are as dry as anthills, and the robins who like to pick through their leavings in the morning seem to have given up all hope of worms. I finally went to the hardware store to buy a sprinkler, partly to save what I could, and partly because I take so much pleasure from watching the robins darting through the edges of the spray, catching insects desperate for moisture. I know their dance is nothing more than survival, but to me it looks exactly like joy.

Turning leaves are ordinarily the loveliest part of this lovely month, but this year the leaves are still green—drooping but green—and the few that have already fallen are brown. The steady September rains they needed for October color never materialized. Some places in this region measured .02 inches of rain last month, I hear, but at our house we got none.

And yet the light is nevertheless October light, one of the seasonal triggers that tells migratory birds when it's time to move on. More than 650 bird species nest in North America, and more than half of those species migrate. Living in their flight path is another pleasure of this season, never mind that much of the migration happens at night. I can sometimes hear them passing high above, impossible to see.

These days I stand at the window every chance I get to watch the last of the ruby-throated hummingbirds drinking from the feeders. It's a predictable rite of autumn, more regular, these days, than rain. In years past, the last hummingbird arrived in my yard during the second week of October, and there is no reason to believe that this year will be any different.

THE COMFORT OF CROWS

In August the resident hummingbird wars are fierce, so violent that I've seen one bird knock another to the ground. The travelers are much less inclined to quarrel, too tired or too intent on conserving energy to engage in battle. They rest, one at a time, on the feeder's perch. They drink and drink and drink. Then they lift into the air, weightless, and take cover again in a nearby tree. One day they will leave and be gone for good. But no matter how long I stand at the window and watch, I never know which time will be the very last.

The Butterfly Cage

Fall ✤ *Week 5*

They seemed to understand what my husband and I had
known for quite some time: even wings can't guarantee a
smooth flight.

—AIMEE NEZHUKUMATATHIL, *World of Wonders*

I bought the mesh enclosure from a guy on the internet who
teaches monarch enthusiasts how to "raise the migration," but
monarchs raised indoors, it turns out, are weaker than their wild
sisters and brothers and therefore less likely to survive the migration. They are also more likely to pass along weaker genes, perhaps
because they are not subjected to the usual winnowing forces of
nature before they reproduce. I put my butterfly cage in the attic
after I read that report. I never want to be party to making things
worse.

There's a brilliance to the bloody, perilous world. Sometimes the
creatures who survive are the fittest. Sometimes they are merely the
luckiest, the ones who set off on their journey at a time when there
is *not* a hurricane brewing in the Gulf of Mexico, the ones whose
route takes them through ragged, unkempt stretches of landscape
where milkweed still grows, instead of through sterile suburban

wastelands or miles of monoculture farms. Left to its own wisdom, nature normally works these things out, with the lucky or strong butterflies outnumbering the weak or unlucky ones. Beyond planting even more milkweed, I vowed not to interfere again. No monarch caterpillars appeared on my milkweed the next year or the next, and their absence made it easy to keep my promise.

Then one day, well into October, I stooped to get a closer look at a butterfly in my pollinator garden, trying to see whether it was a black swallowtail or a spicebush swallowtail or maybe a dark-morph eastern tiger swallowtail, all of whom are too similar in appearance for someone with my imperfect eyesight to tell apart, especially when they're flying from flower to flower. I was eye-level with the parsley I'd planted in the flower bed, hoping to attract black swallowtails, and that's when I noticed a dozen or more black-and-yellow caterpillars chewing away on the leaves. Black swallowtail babies!

I was exultant. It had been a terrible year for pollinators in this yard. Perhaps the long, cool spring delayed their emergence. Perhaps the cold spell in early summer killed too many of them. And perhaps my neighbors' mosquito-killing services had delivered the coup de grâce, wiping out any survivors of those late frosts. But here, at last, were butterflies—a few adults and a whole host of offspring colonizing my parsley.

When I checked the next morning, though, there were fewer caterpillars. Later that afternoon, fewer still. Caterpillars are camouflaged and also adept at hiding—I have "lost" monarch caterpillars safely enclosed in a butterfly cage—so I wasn't particularly worried. The bluebirds nesting in the box a few yards away, or the crows stalking the perimeter, might have grabbed a caterpillar or two, but butterflies are profligate. A single black swallowtail female can lay up to fifty eggs each day. Even songbird predation doesn't generally wipe out an entire brood.

But the next morning, there were only three caterpillars left on my parsley: two tiny ones busily eating, and a bigger one that was curiously still. When I looked more closely, I saw that it was dead, and when I rocked back on my heels to ponder what might've happened, a red wasp glided over to the parsley and showed me: it was carrying away pieces of caterpillar to feed its own young.

I didn't even think about it. I pinched off the leaf where the two surviving caterpillars, oblivious to danger, were munching away. I brought them with me into the house and set them, leaf and all, on my writing table. Then I sat down to conduct a raging internal debate.

On the one hand, interference with natural processes is nearly always a mistake, and not just with caterpillars. I have made this mistake again and again, and I ought to have learned my lesson by this late date. "Thou shouldst not have been old till thou hadst been wise," the court fool tells an aging Lear. Someone needs to say those words to me every day of my life.

On the other hand, natural systems aren't natural anymore. Even the most desolate landscapes on Earth have human fingerprints all over them. In the context of a planet's suffering, the impulse to bring in a few caterpillars and raise them safe from wasps and poisons is hardly an environmental crime. I can't reverse the ravages of climate change, but *this* caterpillar? I can save this one.

OK, but how? Cool weather slows caterpillar development, so moving them indoors, away from the heat and sunlight of the flower bed, would be to risk releasing them into the first frost of the year. Caterpillar season ought to be over by October. Swallowtail chrysalids can safely overwinter in a year of normal weather, but we no longer have normal winters. To be sure these caterpillars could grow up and fly away before the cold weather came, I needed to leave them outside.

Which is how the giant butterfly cage in the attic came to be the giant butterfly cage in a sheltered corner of our back deck. Fortunately, Haywood's container garden, planted for the humans in the house to eat, always includes a heavy planter of parsley. He didn't hesitate to repurpose it for caterpillars and installed it in the bottom of the butterfly cage, where the planter's heft offered the corollary benefit of preventing the cage from blowing over in a storm. It would not keep predators from tearing the screen open, however. I could only hope the birds and raccoons and opossums would decline to venture so close to the house. The smell of dog on the deck might help.

The swallowtail caterpillars were lucky. Every morning I checked, and every morning the screen was still intact, the caterpillars were still eating, and the parsley was diminishing before my eyes. The hot fall days and the plentiful parsley soon worked their astonishing, ordinary magic. I wasn't there to see it, but both caterpillars transformed themselves into chrysalids. They looked like unassuming brown leaves attached to a parsley stem by a slender filament of silk.

One of the filaments proved too delicate to hold during a pounding rain, but the other! Oh, the other transformed itself anew, breaking open, parting, unfolding. I wasn't there for that miracle, either—by the time I checked again, the butterfly, a female, was slowly opening and closing her wings—but I was there for the next one. I unzipped the cage and reached inside. She climbed onto my hand and waited while I brought her past the screen. Then she lifted herself into the air, up and over the roof and into the sky.

This one caterpillar. This one butterfly.

Praise Song for
Sleeping Bees

The nights are cool now. The ground is glistening, and the night is glistening, too, just beginning to lighten. With every step, I leave footprints in the dew. It is early, and chill. Creatures of the diurnal world are still sleeping, and creatures of the nocturnal world are looking for a safe place to sleep.

I have abandoned all hope of sleeping and have crept outside to watch the bumblebees sleep instead. As night comes on, they crawl into the balsam flowers, those colorful bells of red and purple and pink. I love to see them sheltering from the rain beneath a giant canna leaf, but I especially love to see them sleep, their fuzzy bumblebutts poking out of the blossoms. It comforts me to know my garden is full of sleeping bees.

I brush the edge of a flower—barely touching it, an innocent accident—but the bee is angry, unforgiving. She backs out of her bed and rears back. She waves her bumblebee arms and buzzes at me.

I squat to look at her, careful not to touch, but she does not trust me. She knows I belong to the lumbering kind, the true bumbling trouble at the heart of the world.

Holiness

Fall ❧ Week 6

Come unto me, all ye that labour and are heavy laden, and
I will give you rest.

—MATTHEW 11:28

My great-grandmother was a lifelong Baptist who spent the
last four decades of her life worshiping with the Methodists
because by then there was only one church left in her community.
Mother Ollie gladly attended Mass at my family's Catholic church
in Birmingham, too, but she never drifted from her quiet adher-
ence to the King James ways of her youth.

She was so quiet in her convictions that I was ten or twelve
before I noticed that she went straight back to her room after
church every Sunday. On other days, she was busy—shelling peas
or snapping beans, crocheting or quilting or sewing—but on
Sunday her hands fell still, and her sewing machine sat silent. The
foot-pedal Singer she'd ordered from a catalog sometime during
the early twentieth century was in daily use until a few weeks
before her death in 1982, but she never sewed on Sunday.

When I went looking for her help with a tatting project one
Sunday afternoon, I found out why. Tatting is a kind of lace made

of tight knots tied in very fine string. The trick is to tie the right kind of knot without tangling the string into the wrong kind, but I had made so many of the wrong knots that I couldn't figure out how to unpick the tangle and start again. I found Mother Ollie sitting in a chair under the window, her Bible in her lap. The book was old, with edges so worn they curved inward toward the pages, as soft as a puppy. I knocked on the open door. "Mother Ollie, can you help me with this?"

All these years later, I think about the ache it must have caused my great-grandmother, the one whose bedroom I shared whenever the house was full, to disappoint—even in this slight way—a child she loved so much. But that day she could not help me with my needlework. "Not today, honey," she said. "The Lord tells us not to work on the Sabbath." And handwork, by definition, is work.

I've thought of that conversation many times over the years. Sunday has never been a day of rest for me. I've always used at least part of the day to catch up with work, with laundry, with grocery shopping, with the Hydra of email. People tend to imagine that the life of a writer is mainly a matter of mooning around, waiting for ideas to bubble up, or sitting down with a beautiful pen and an elegant notebook, recording the fruits of inspiration. But no. Most writers I know spend more time writing responses to email than anything else.

I started devoting Sunday afternoons to email almost as soon as it was invented because I realized that emailing on a Sunday, when offices were closed, meant a reply wouldn't come flying right back to me, creating the need to answer yet another email. But I don't know anyone who takes Sunday off anymore. These days, emailing someone about a work matter on Sunday isn't any different from emailing them on Monday.

And yet it's not as though the world stopped on Sunday in the Lower Alabama of my childhood. The crops—and the weeds—in my grandfather's fields continued to grow, whatever the day. My grandmother still had papers to grade and lessons to plan. The peas in the bushel basket on the back porch would not shell themselves. Nevertheless, my people put their work aside on Sunday to nap on the daybed or sit on the porch and rock. They didn't ask themselves, as I do, whether they could "afford" to rest. God obliged them to rest, and so they rested.

There are many, many people for whom this kind of Sabbath is not an option. People who work double shifts—or double jobs—just to make ends meet truly can't afford to rest, but I could reorganize my life if I tried. I could focus on priorities, spend less time on things that matter little to me and make more time for those that matter most. Somehow, over the years, I had simply learned to live without feeling permitted to rest.

That changed after my first book tour, a series of bookstore stops around the country for a book that didn't appear until I was already fifty-seven years old. Possibly I was just too old by then to learn the art of solo travel: of lying in a different bed night after night and actually sleeping, of finding my way through new cities and new airport terminals. I love meeting book people with all my heart, but all my body was in revolt by the time I got home.

I sat on the sofa with my laptop, planning to get started on the ninety million emails that had piled up in my absence, but instead I fell asleep. I tried the wing chair next to the sofa with no better results. When I found myself looking at the one clear spot on my desk as a good place to lay my head, I gave up and went to bed, rousing myself barely in time for supper. Then I slept eleven hours more.

The commandments don't identify by name which day of the week should be the Sabbath. They don't even mention the need to attend church. "Remember the sabbath day, to keep it holy," reads Mother Ollie's Bible. "Six days shalt thou labor, and do all thy work: But the seventh day is the sabbath of the Lord thy God: in it thou shalt not do any work."

Reading those verses again made me wonder: What if resting, all by itself, is the real act of holiness? What if honoring the gift of our only life in this gorgeous world means taking time every week to slow down? To sleep? To breathe? The natural world has never needed us more than it needs us now, but we can't be of much use to it if we remain in a perpetual state of exhaustion and despair.

It's hard *not* to work on Sunday, but I do try. I take a walk around my favorite lake, the best possible way to celebrate a day of rest in autumn, when the temperatures have finally dropped, the rains have finally come, and Middle Tennessee is serving up one fine day after another.

In fall, the beautyberries gleam in all their purple ripeness beside the last of the asters and the snakeroot flowers. Behind its mother, a fawn forages, its springtime spots beginning to fade. A great blue heron stands on a downed tree at the edge of the water, preening each damp, curling feather and sorting it into place. Every year a fallen log just off the trail boasts a majestic crop of chicken of the woods, and the seedpods of the redbud trees are ready to burst. The crows are talking in the treetops, and the sound of a lone cricket invariably rises up from the skein of vegetation next to the lake. I never fail to stop and listen. Its song is as beautiful and as heart-lifting as any hymn.

Praise Song for Forgetfulness

"I have emails from 2019 still waiting for an answer," I tell my friend the priest. It is not a confession, but it might as well be. I feel terrible about those unanswered emails. There are many hundreds of newer unanswered emails, too—I could spend all day, every day, answering emails and never catch up—but the longer they wait, the worse I feel.

Perhaps it is a confession after all, for my friend is raising his hands in benediction. He is mumbling words in Latin. "Are you absolving me of the sin of unanswered emails?" I ask.

"Yes," he says, smiling. He is joking, but I feel better.

And then I remember the squirrels. All day long, they are harvesting acorns and hiding them in places they fully expect to remember. I find them constantly. Some of the acorns are hidden in knotholes, and some are tucked beneath the birdbath, but most are planted in the ground. Squirrels take care in planting: digging to the right depth, covering the acorn, and patting the loose soil until it is tucked in just so. Squirrels have a prodigious memory for where they have hidden their stores, but they don't remember them all.

There are worse things, I think, than leaving a task undone. The oak forests of the world would not exist if squirrels did not lose track of acorns.

Because I Can't Stop
Drinking in the Light

Fall ❧ Week 7

How I linger now in the light! The shadows at day's end grow long and then longer, and the dry soil throws out motes of dust that catch in the sunset and seem to burst into flame. It is late in coming, but autumn is on fire—sourwood and red maple and poison sumac and witch hazel and oakleaf hydrangea. The red berries of the dogwood trees and the red seedpods of the magnolias flare up, too, and so do the berries of the bush honeysuckle, invasive but beautiful in the failing light.

This is crow light. Light that gleams on glossy black feathers and makes of the crow a breathing shadow, a living, winging, crow-talking god. The light that renders a crow incandescent in the afternoon is the same light that only minutes later tenders the gift of twilight, when colors fade and all the world becomes a crow.

Into this light come the human children, finally home from school and all the obligations that attend childhood in the suburbs: soccer practice and guitar lessons and math tutorials and martial arts and I don't know what else—it's impossible to keep track of what suburban parents believe is necessary for a child to learn even after the child has spent all day learning. But the children are home by crow light and free at last to play with one another, setting their own rules and settling their own disputes.

My children were part of an earlier after-school herd that migrated from yard to yard, football giving way to tag as five o'clock became five thirty, too dark to see the ball. Now those boys are men, and even the younger children who followed their trackless ways through the neighborhood are grown. But there will always be new children playing in the last light, and their glad, galloping games and their high, thin voices lift my heart. I try to time my walk to hear them play.

This is the final week for such autumn pleasures, though, for on Sunday the clocks will change again. It will be too dark to play by the time the children get home, and the yards will be empty when Rascal and I take our walk after my own day's work is done.

Americans live in an age of disputes, so it should come as no surprise when fury erupts over this question of clocks. Even so, I am always surprised when I utter some expression of regret about the coming time change in the presence of someone who, it turns out, prefers her light to arrive before breakfast. You would think I was expressing a preference for strychnine in my coffee. My preferences don't matter in any case. Except for Arizona and Hawaii, which haven't adopted daylight saving time and so never sprang forward in the first place, the clocks will fall back an hour on the first Sunday after Halloween, and circadian rhythms will be disrupted across the land.

Wild animals, who have learned our patterns and adjusted their own in response, will try to cross the road at the wrong time of day, and more of them than usual will lose their lives in the confusion. Always, after a time change, even more of my wild neighbors lose their lives.

Human babies will continue to wake before dawn, only now they will wake their bleary-eyed parents a full hour earlier than the day before.

Dogs will demand their supper at the usual hour, and their people will spend the next hour fruitlessly trying to convince them that it is not in fact suppertime.

And I will take my day's-end walk in the dark, missing the sunset and the sounds of children calling to one another as they play.

Fig. 115.

Fig. 116.

Fig. 117.

SPIRAL

The Lazarus Snail

Fall ❧ Week 8

One has to respect the preferences of another creature, no matter its size.

—ELISABETH TOVA BAILEY, *The Sound of a Wild Snail Eating*

D amp. That's the thing about a forest in fall that feels very different from a forest in summer. Even when hair-dryer heat is due to arrive later in the day, by October the mornings are cooler, almost restful, a balm to hot and thirsty souls. When November comes, if the autumn showers arrive as they ought, seeping into the soil and permeating the leaves, a forest becomes the liminal space where land and sky come together: the dew lingers longer in the morning, and the trees hold on to the clouds, stitching them to the earth, pulling them closer to the ground.

This was the dreamy state of things on the Cumberland Plateau when Haywood and I borrowed the cabin for our last visit of the year.

Rain was in the forecast for our weekend away, so I packed ten or twelve books to give myself options. I like to see books spread out on a table like a banquet. Every time I pass by, I'm tempted to sit down and begin something delicious, or to pick up where I left off the last time I played hooky from work, the work that colonizes most of the rooms in our own house.

The rain held off for the first day of our trip, but it came in torrents during the second night, bringing thumb-sized acorns from the mighty chestnut oaks hammering down on the metal roof. Rascal sent up an alarm at each fresh disturbance, refusing to abandon his post even when we tried to tell him all was well. This rescue dog's prior life apparently did not include a rainstorm in a cabin with a metal roof during a mast year for chestnut oaks.

By morning the rain had settled into a sleepy murmur, and the trees were filled with fog. Perhaps that's why I picked up *The Sound of a Wild Snail Eating* instead of one of the brightly colored novels I'd brought, or one of the thick nonfiction books that promised crucial information. It was a cool, rainy day in autumn, and I was snug in a log cabin on a windswept bluff. I wanted to be absorbed in a story of wildness that was also a story of love.

The Sound of a Wild Snail Eating is Elisabeth Tova Bailey's account of being felled by a debilitating illness. Except for visits from a caregiver and the occasional friend, she spends all day in bed. Her one companion is a small woodland snail whose home base is a pot of field violets at her bedside. As the months of illness creep by, Bailey learns to recognize her mollusk companion's interests and preferences, to understand that the snail is every bit the individual she is herself. "The life of a snail is as full of tasty food, comfortable beds of sorts, and a mix of pleasant and not-so-pleasant adventures as that of anyone I know," she writes.

All that long, drizzly day I read on the dry porch while Haywood read in the gazebo on the bluff. The fog down in the cove coalesced into a sinewy creature made from mist, coiling through the valley, retracting, and then rolling forward again. Gusts of wind sent acorns clattering onto the roof and raindrops filtering through the screen. It struck me that to sit on a porch in the rainy woods is a bit like *being* a snail: inside and outside at once, at home in the wet world.

But the dog, who had finally grown accustomed to the explosions of acorn projectiles, had not grown accustomed to the stillness of a rainy Sunday afternoon. For Rascal, being stuck indoors, especially with his humans immersed in their books, is an invitation to mischief. When he shook himself and hopped off the swing to begin a reconnaissance of entertainment opportunities, I watched to make sure he wasn't about to grab something precious to our friends and tear around the house with it in a game of keep-away, a game I always lose. Fortunately, the intriguing smells and sounds on the porch seemed to obviate any impulse he might have had to chew up a family Bible.

I really couldn't tell you how long he had been tossing the acorn into the air and pouncing on it, carrying it around in his mouth and then spitting it out, over and over again, before I noticed what he was doing. I also couldn't say how long it was before he brought the acorn over and set it next to my feet, but that's when I glanced down and wondered, "Wait, *is* that an acorn?"

If you can believe it, Rascal's plaything was not an acorn. It was a snail. A snail so dry, despite the humid air, that it felt nearly weightless. A snail with no sign of an occupant. Less snail than shell.

I picked it up and carried it indoors to peer at it beneath the better light of a lamp. It was difficult to say for sure, but I thought I could see something in there, something desiccated and still.

I did not take the snail outside and set it in the mossy, acorn-strewn soil, which is what I should have done. Instead I started casting about for some way to approximate Elisabeth Tova Bailey's woodland-violet habitat. My eye fell upon a decorative flowerpot where my friend had planted some sort of succulent. The potting mixture was so dry and firm that I wasn't sure it contained any real dirt, or even whether the succulent was a real plant. Nevertheless, I took the pot to the kitchen sink and gave it a good soaking. Then I set the snail gently beneath the succulent.

Looking back, I recognize this whole operation as one of those exercises in guilt abeyance that Catholic school engenders in a certain sort of girl. If I had done nothing for the snail, or the former snail, and simply given the dog back his plaything, there was a decent chance I'd wake up at three o'clock in the morning wondering what might have happened if I had tried to save it. And it was so perfectly suited to its woodland home that if I had taken it outside and left it among the fallen leaves, I would never have been able to find it again. Not knowing whether the snail was alive was just as likely to torment me at three in the morning as giving up on it without trying. I confess—confession also being a holdover of Catholic school—that I was proceeding much more with the goal of preserving my own peace of mind than in saving this porch-entrapped snail who, as far as I knew, might have perished under a wicker settee months ago.

Holding out no real hope for the snail's resurrection, I gave the dog a chew toy and went back to my book, where I began to read about the marvelous shell-regenerative capacities of snails and their ability to survive long periods, even years, of dormancy during inhospitable conditions. Even then, I did not walk over to the succulent pot and check on the snail. It was an hour or more before a break in the rain made me put my book down, determined to get in a walk before the sky opened up again. Rascal was already leashed and dancing at my feet when I glanced over at the succulent. As I have mentioned, what catches my eye is always movement, never an object at rest, but something about the side of the pot, textured and mottled though it was, made me stop. And then stoop to look.

The snail was halfway down the side of the pot, fully extended. Its four tentacles—two above and two shorter ones below, just as Bailey describes—were reaching forward, and its foot was stretched out, trailing behind. All of it was visibly damp, the usual state of a healthy snail. Its whorled shell now glistened with life. Even when I bent close, the snail carried on with its getaway, though at a speed that made movement nearly undetectable.

I was so shocked I dropped the leash. Then I hurried the pot outside, snail and all, and tucked it under the dripping leaves of a low-growing laurel.

There is something almost unseemly about the idea of rushing a snail back into the rain, for clearly the snail is not a creature accustomed to hurry, but some part of me always panics at the possibility of causing a wild animal harm. In my urgency to remove myself, to step away before I can blunder into trouble, I set up the exact conditions into which trouble so often blooms. And who knows what damage Rascal had already inflicted on this poor snail who only wanted to get back to the soil and the rain.

I had the same insistent need for haste when I went to clean out the nest box the house wrens used last spring. House wrens are hell on bluebird nests, puncturing eggs and killing the nestlings if the parents leave them unguarded, so I had delayed cleaning out the box, hoping to encourage the prolific wrens to build their next nest somewhere else. But house wrens are fleet and furtive, and they had started a new clutch in the old nest before I noticed.

When I opened the box and pulled the nest out, the baby wrens lifted their heads and gaped at me. My heart leaped so instantly I almost leaped myself. I was terrified that I'd destroyed their home, but instead of proceeding with deliberation, careful to return the nest undamaged, I shoved it back into the box and slammed the hinged wall closed. My heart didn't stop pounding for a long time, and I didn't feel truly safe until the second clutch had fledged and it was time to clean out the box in earnest. Only after I pulled the nest out again and saw no dead baby birds in the bottom could I take a deep breath.

And that is what a house wren has in common with a woodland snail: I don't want to hurt either one, even by accident. Which is why I set the snail down under that laurel and headed back up the stairs.

I like to send photos of interesting things that happen at the cabin to our generous friends, but it wasn't until I was on the porch that I thought, "I should take a picture of the snail in its natural habitat." I clomped down the steps again, this time with my phone. The barest moment had passed, but when I reached the laurel, the snail was gone, vanished into that dripping, fog-drenched forest.

Praise Song for
a Larger Home

After our last child left for college, I struggled. The full life it had taken years, decades, to build had vanished, as evanescent as the mist. They all came home for Thanksgiving, and I—who had spent so much of their childhood despairing that I would never again have a moment to myself—followed them around like a girl spurned but loving still, ashamed.

They are building their own lives now, and when they left home to return to them, I took myself to the woods. Because sometimes the only cure for homesickness is to enlarge the definition of home.

How to Rake Leaves
on a Windy Day

Fall ✤ *Week 9*

It's the season I often mistake / Birds for leaves, and leaves
for birds.

—ADA LIMÓN, *The Hurting Kind*

L eaf blowers are like giant whining insects that have moved
into your skull. They are swarming behind your eyes, drilling
down into your teeth. Leaf blowers have ruined autumn with their
insistent drone and their noxious fumes, and they are everywhere.
You may believe it is futile to resist them, but you can resist them.
In almost every situation where something is loud, obnoxious, and
seemingly ubiquitous, resistance is an option.

Head to the toolshed in your backyard and fiddle with the rusty
padlock until it finally yields. Reach into the corner where you
keep the shovel and the posthole digger and the pruning shears.
From that jumble of wonderful tools requiring no gasoline, pull
out a rake. It has been quite some time since you needed to clear a
space for kickball games, so you have given over more and more of
your yard to wildness. For this reason, it has also been quite some
time since you last used the rake.

It reminds you of the comb your mother tugged gently through your clean hair after a bath. Think of the way your mother smelled as she leaned close to untangle the snarls. Remember how your damp hair held the rows the comb left behind, like new-planted peanuts in your grandfather's fields. That's what the raked paths in the yard will look like after you've cleared them of leaves.

Let the leaves lie everywhere it is possible to let the leaves lie. You aren't trying for clean lines; you are trying only to pacify the angry neighbor who complained because some of your leaves blew into her yard. Leave the leaves in the flower beds. Leave them close to the house and around the raised roots of trees, beneath the woody shrubs, in the margins of the yard. Leave them in all the places you have left to your wild neighbors. The tall grass and the dried stems of wildflowers are where crawling things are hiding, sheltering under the layers of leaves. When the birds return in springtime, these insects will be a feast for their nestlings. Whatever it might feel like on this damp November day, remind yourself that springtime is coming.

Don't let the wind become a frustration to you. In a forest, fallen leaves compost themselves to feed the trees. The leaves you let sit today will molder and rot through the winter, generating their own heat and protecting large trees and small creatures alike. Think of your desultory raking as a way to feed the trees, as an investment in the urban forest. If your neighbor complains again, tell her you are feeding her trees.

When the wind rises, stand still. This is your chance to smell the living soil stirred up by raking. Its pungent scent may recall to you the long-ago taste of mud pies.

While you're breathing in the scent of ancient soil, listen for the squirrels. They will be fussing at you from the treetops, scolding you for stirring up the dirt they have claimed for their own planting. All autumn long, the squirrels have been sowing acorns across the landscape. Take a moment, standing with your rake, to wonder how many forests the squirrels' thumbless hands have planted in all the busy autumns of their kind.

See? For a moment you have managed to forget the leaf blowers! You have failed to note the sounds of traffic on the nearby street where everyone is in a hurry and always drives too fast. For a moment, too, you have forgotten your worries—your own private worries and the bigger worries of the world.

Remember that one day soon the wind will die down, and the creatures that live beneath the leaf litter will burrow into the cold ground. For now, give yourself over to what is happening in the sky. Watch the last leaves unloose themselves from their branches and deliver themselves to the wind. Watch the wind, which you cannot see, catch and lift the leaves, which you can. Watch the wind catch them, lift them, drop them, and lift them again.

Before you go inside, take a leaf into your hand. Put it on your desk or next to your bed. Keep it nearby, through whatever troubles the long winter brings. It will help you remember that nothing is truly over. It will help you remember what the wind always teaches us in autumn: that just because you can't see something doesn't mean it isn't there.

The Mast Year

Fall ❧ Week 10

There is much going on in your yard that would not be
going if you didn't have one or more oak trees gracing
your piece of planet earth.

—Douglas W. Tallamy, *The Nature of Oaks*

I t's been a poor year for acorns in this yard, though it's been a
mast year for nearly every other kind of fruiting and seed-bearing
plant. A cool, wet spring and a hot summer gentled by late rains,
the kind of weather we haven't seen in years, left the pokeweed
plants weighted with purple berries, the redbud limbs heavy with
seedpods, the hollies covered with ripening fruit. Even the new
cedars are dotted here and there with drupes. I planted them for
the flock of cedar waxwings that overwinters here, but they are
young trees, and the local songbirds will likely clear out the berries
before the waxwings arrive.

My mother's standard measure for a new plant's growth—"the
first year they sleep; the second year they creep; the third year they
leap"—still holds. This is the year the cedars are supposed to creep,
and next year I can look for a decent crop of drupes. Plenty for the
local birds and the cedar waxwings alike. Plenty for everyone.

From time to time, woodland trees and plants will break out into a glorious mast year, a season during which they produce an especially bountiful harvest. I had been expecting a mast year for the white oak just outside our bedroom window, but it produced almost no acorns this fall. White oaks generally mast every two to five years. Last year brought a poor yield, and the year before that was poor as well. I thought surely this year of good rain would also bring a good crop of acorns.

It takes a lot out of a tree to produce so many seeds. No one knows exactly why trees mast, though it may have something to do with producing more food than wildlife can consume, thus giving the tree's offspring a better chance of survival. A mast year allows more animals to survive, as well, and this year there are not so many chipmunks and squirrels as there are when our oak tree masts. The blue jays seem to be doing well—they show up at my feeder as soon as I leave a fresh batch of peanuts in the tray—but they don't hang around the yard the way they do when acorns are plentiful. There is nothing a blue jay loves better than an acorn. A blue jay, caching acorns many decades ago, may have planted this very oak.

The oak has been standing here since before our house was built, back to when this yard was still a forest. The other trees were planted in 1948 by our late backdoor neighbor, Joe, a lineman for the telephone company who came home from World War II to buy the very first house built in our neighborhood. Joe and his wife, Millie, lived downslope from the scraped lot where our house would stand two years later, and Joe was concerned about erosion. Maple trees have shallow roots that stabilize the soil, and Joe planted eighteen sugar maple saplings here, hoping to keep our soil in our yard and out of his storm cellar.

The maples' shallow roots have cost a few of them their lives. Joe and Millie lived out sixty-five years of happy marriage in the house behind ours, but after they died, a developer tore it down, taking no care to protect the trees Joe left behind. And because tree roots don't respect property lines, some of the builder's heavy equipment and some of his piles of brick and lumber got dumped on roots that fed trees in our yard. I've been trying to replace the trees we lost ever since.

Planting a tree is a gesture of faith in the future. One year we put in new hollies and serviceberries, new southern arrowwoods. Another year it was a dogwood and a sweetbay magnolia, and the year before that a red maple sapling that came by mail from Walden Pond. Most recently it was bottlebrush buckeyes and three different varieties of pawpaws. I am already thinking about what I'll order next year from my list of native plants our yard still lacks. A persimmon, maybe, or a Kentucky coffeetree? Both?

It's impossible to keep pace with all the trees that have been cut down, and all the trees that have died of stress, during construction in this suddenly prosperous neighborhood. A wonderful old shingle oak across the street is dying, and the new neighbors, the ones who bought the grand house that rose in place of the modest rental where my mother lived during her final years, have not noticed yet. The tree is at the street, nowhere near the house, but the builder must have found its roots inconvenient in some way. I watched one day as three workers hacked out a major root and poured concrete into the hole where it had been. Later, a dump truck deposited soil over the concrete, and a landscaping crew installed sod on top of the dirt. Well, first they treated the soil with a pre-emergent poison to keep wildflower seeds from gaining purchase. *Then* they covered it with sod.

I wonder if my oak's poor yield is tied to this slow-motion devastation, if somewhere a white oak that once lived in a now barren yard was lost without my noticing. A white oak that through the years had been my own oak's mate, its pollen carried here on the wind.

Sometimes trees pop up, seemingly from nowhere, as gifts from the birds. We protect a volunteer black locust and a volunteer red mulberry as tenderly as any nursery-bought seedling. A volunteer hackberry already reaches to the power line. Soon we will run out of room at the margins and be forced to set seedlings down right in the middle of our yard, wherever there is space between the trees that are already here. The neighbor who does not like our leaves once told me we should cut down most of our trees. "They're so thick it feels like the house can't breathe," she said.

"That's because it can't," I said. "But the trees can breathe."

That's what I think I said, anyway. Maybe I only wanted to say it and didn't have the nerve.

At the base of each new tree, Haywood sets a five-gallon bucket with a hole he drilled into the bottom. This was my mother's approach for keeping young plants alive, a poor man's drip-irrigation system. The slow release of water allows the tree's roots time to take up moisture. As it grows, Haywood moves the bucket farther out, coaxing the roots to reach, giving them a reason to set themselves firmly into the earth. Once a tree is well established, it's time to plant another.

Every time a beautiful old tree is lost here, I think of my mother's indignation when the power company cut down a giant pine at the corner of our yard in Birmingham. In its place they put up a massive pole, a bright silver monstrosity more than a foot wide and at least twelve feet high. Mom called the power company every day until someone came out and painted the pole forest green. Around it she planted flowering trees and shrubs that wouldn't grow tall enough to obstruct the power lines but would still disguise the pole. Driving by the house a few years later, you never would have known there was anything ugly within that little grove of dogwoods. In springtime all you noticed were the drifting white flowers and the mockingbird that sang there every morning and every evening and all day long.

I am older now than my mother was when she was harassing the customer-service department of the Alabama Power Company, and more and more I ponder words like *bounty* and *replete* and *enough*. I think of what we are losing from this world and of what we will leave behind when we ourselves are lost. The trees. The stories. The people who love us and who know we love them, who will carry our love into the world after we are gone.

I am remembering again that a family is still a family though they may live in different houses. We see each of our children from time to time, though hardly ever all of them at once. But for Thanksgiving they will be here together, and I am planning all the traditional dishes. We tried to simplify our menu the first pandemic year, when nobody from our extended families could visit, but our sons revolted. They wanted their great-grandmother's squash dressing, which takes two days to make. They wanted their grandmother's pecan pie. They wanted creamed spinach and sweet potato soufflé and lady peas and rolls so soft they can hardly hold the butter. Our children are coming home to gather around the same table for the first time in months, so we will make them a feast. At Thanksgiving, every year is a mast year.

Until then, I will think of my mother's dogwoods as I fill my water buckets, repurposed from carrying to spilling. The next time Haywood and I visit the Cumberland Plateau, I'll gather acorns to plant here and there at our house—in enough different places, I hope, for a few to escape the blue jays. With any luck, some autumn in a year I may not live to see, there will be many acorns.

And Now the Light Is Failing

Fall ✤ Week 11

> If I could attach a small tag to each of the atoms in my body and travel with them backward in time, I would find that those atoms originated in particular stars in the sky. Those exact atoms.
>
> —ALAN LIGHTMAN, *Searching for Stars on an Island in Maine*

The summer solstice has no effect on me. In June, the leafy trees block so much light it's hard to notice such gradual changes in the sky. Even growing shorter, the summer days feel endless. Summer itself feels endless. But if I happened to notice the dwindling light, the loss wouldn't trouble me: the cooler breath of nighttime would make it a cost I'd gladly pay. Besides, night brings lightning bugs—or it used to, before so many people began to drench their yards with poison. Who wouldn't welcome those flashes of brightness under the trees, even if it meant sharing the yard with mosquitoes, too?

Well, that's a lament for another day. On this day, I am thinking again of autumn light. In autumn, it's hard for me to think of anything else, and the light is leaving.

Now that the leaves have dropped from the hardwood trees and the fallen needles have made a golden ring beneath the pines; now that the migrating songbirds have passed us in the night, and the park turtles have hidden themselves in their loamy chambers, and the rattlesnakes on the bluff have found the crevices in the rock where they will sleep through the cold; now that the exaltation of autumn is gone for another year, and the darkness is visibly deeper with every passing afternoon—*now* is when I begin to yearn for the solstice. I am yearning for the light.

Hope is harder to come by these days, and I find hope more easily in brightness. "More light," Goethe famously called on his deathbed, and I understand. In light, there is human companionship, birdsong, a sense—however illusory—of forward motion. In light, the horizon extends before us, a tableau of endless possibility, while darkness allows all manner of doubts to burble up. When we have lost our certainty of purpose, our very understanding of ourselves, we speak of enduring a dark night of the soul. How much easier it is to give in to gloom, even dejection, when it is the darkness that feels endless.

When I was in college, I liked to walk through the fields where the agriculture students practiced their future profession. Mostly I walked alone, desperate for solitude in a crowded life, but sometimes I walked with my beloved writing teacher. For her it was cardiac rehab, a way to grow stronger after heart surgery. For me it was a respite from schoolwork, a chance to watch bluebirds diving for insects from fence posts, to listen to wind blowing across the fallow fields. It was also a chance to talk with Ruth. She was a trusted mentor to many other young writers, and I loved having her all to myself.

On one walk she mentioned her method for managing insomnia. I don't know why it made such an impression on me. I was twenty, an enthusiastic sleeper. I had such a gift for sleep! I once fell asleep at a high school football game, leaning against the warm knees of my friend Mary's older brother, who sat on the bleachers one row up. Still, I listened as Ruth told me how she had learned to surrender to the wakefulness of aging. She had come to realize that fighting it was what made her so tired. If she kept still and calm, if she never paced the house or checked the clock, she sometimes dropped off again. And even when she didn't, she rose feeling almost as rested as if she'd slept. "Maybe I need rest even more than I need sleep," she said.

I think often about that conversation, and not just on restless nights. I am very close to the age Ruth was when she was my teacher, and I'm beginning to believe that her strategy for living with insomnia might work for metaphorical kinds of darkness, too. Instead of fighting it so hard, maybe I should be honest, tell myself the brutal truth: *This is the world as it is. This is what we've made of it, and there is no going back. This is the best the living world will ever be, and that's only if we can stop the worst from coming.*

I'm not saying I've surrendered. I would never surrender. I'm only talking about a temporary ceasefire. Remember the story about the Christmas Day truce during World War I, when German soldiers and English soldiers held their fire, against official policy on both sides, and sang Christmas carols to one another? That's the kind of ceasefire I mean. The kind where there's a moment to take a breath. A moment for singing. What would life even *be* without singing?

I can't make the hollies stop blooming in November. I can't tell the bluebirds there's no time left for another clutch of eggs even if the temperature has settled into the eighties here in December. They don't know the heat is fleeting, but fretting ensures the survival of not one baby bird.

During my own sleepless nights, I have learned to think of rest as a form of waiting, a state that is both passive and active, resisting the urge to predict but prepared nonetheless for whatever might come.

The night sky is full of stars best seen from a dark place. I try to remember that, too.

Praise Song for
Dead Leaves

Save the saw-toothed leaves of the beeches, every last leaf is on the ground now. Large leaves and small leaves, red leaves and orange leaves and yellow leaves and brown leaves and spotted leaves. All have lost their lavish color and taken on some shade of December, gray or ash or brown.

Above the earth, the moon lights your way. The sky is brighter now, the stars brighter and closer and clearer, but the castanets of fallen leaves are the gift of winter. Hear how they give away the tiniest brown bird, how they reveal the quickest mouse or vole, sounding larger than it will ever be in life. Among the leaves they are all larger than life. Hear the way you yourself sound magnificent, how huge you become with every step on this leafy path, how you grow with every crunch and rustle, how you rise with every crackle and break.

Almost like you belong here.

ANGLES ALTERNITE &
OPPOSITE   HEXAGON   *Fig.24.*

Ode to a Dark Season

Fall ⚘ Week 12

The day breaks with little help from birds.

—ALDO LEOPOLD, *A Sand County Almanac*

T o walk in any well-managed forest during December is to confront the inevitability of death.

This is the month of blank, lowering skies, when the last of the leaves lift and drift into a drizzly wind. Seasonal cues aren't always reliable in this changing climate, when heat so often clings through the fall, and I feared there would be no color at all this year. I was wrong. The sugar maples went golden at last, though not in October. This year they glowed against gray November skies, each leaf giving off its own light.

The understory at the park has died back now, and the contours of the land are evident once more. In December I can see the places where rainwater flows downhill to find Otter Creek, then the Little Harpeth River, and someday—winding through the Mississippi River watershed—the Gulf of Mexico. In summer, the forest keeps the journey of rainwater a secret, tucks it away under a tangle of green, just as it keeps hidden all the songbird nests that are so visible now against a pewter sky.

The birds themselves have largely fallen silent, their summer-time music giving way to sharper calls of warning whenever a hawk is near. The hawks are always hunting on these cloudy days when they can fly without casting a shadow, but the chipmunks hear the blue jays' warning jeer and take note. They stand upright, their forefeet clutched to their chests, to take up the cry. Soon the quiet trees are echoing with an unearthly sound that always seems far too loud to have emerged from chipmunk lips.

A late autumn drizzle transforms the woods into an astonish-ment, but almost everything else about this time of year feels mournful to me. Perhaps because this is the season when my father's cancer stopped responding to treatment, and when, a decade later, my beloved mother-in-law entered hospice care. Perhaps it is only because I am growing older myself. I feel the throb of time more acutely with every passing autumn.

One year that feeling was complicated by a routine medical screening. As I waited for the doctor to call with the pathology report that would clarify whether our long family history of cancer had finally caught up with me, I looked up the preliminary diag-nosis online and scared myself to death. I mentioned this turn of events in an email to a friend who would understand—she is my age, and she had just lost her mother to their own family history of sudden cardiac arrest. "I feel like I've reached the age when I have to make friends with death," she wrote back. "I want to cultivate more of my mother's fearless embrace of death, though I'm not at all sure how to go about that."

I think about her words as I walk each day through this sepia world of autumn. I think, too, of the poet John Keats, whose odes were so bound up in the evanescent nature of time, "the weariness, the fever, and the fret" of human life. I know what he meant when he wrote that "to think is to be full of sorrow / And leaden-eyed despairs."

I have not yet found my way to being "half in love with easeful Death," as Keats was. When my doctor called to say the biopsy had come back with no sign of malignancy, relief swept through me like a high autumn wind. Never mind that such news is only ever a reprieve.

Maybe it was the sudden sense of death dislodged, however temporarily, that made me look at the small, seasonal deaths around me with a feeling of kinship. Fallen leaves soften the path I walk on, but not for my sake. The leaves fall to feed the trees, to shelter the creatures who are essential to this forest in a way that I will never be. The misty rain unstiffens deadwood, making places for nesting woodpeckers to excavate next spring. I can stop to count the rings of shelf fungi on a dead tree and know how long they have been growing, how long the death of the tree has been feeding the life of the forest.

So much life springs from all this death that to spend time in the woods is also to contemplate *im*mortality. On the way out of the park I passed a red-tailed hawk lying at the base of a power pole, apparently electrocuted, its perfect wing extended in death. The vultures were already beginning to circle as I passed. I drove on, knowing what would come next, what always comes next: death to life, earth to air, wing to wing.

December reminds us that the membrane between life and death is permeable, an endless back and forth that makes something of everything, no matter how small, no matter how transitory. To be impermanent is only one part of life. There will always be a resurrection.

The Thing with Feathers

Fall ❧ *Week 13*

Winter is almost here. We haven't had a hard freeze yet, but the Yankee robins have returned from their nesting grounds up north to join the local robins in big, noisy flocks that rival the starlings for boisterous debate. The stars shine more precisely in the cold sky.

Though the nights are chill, the days are mostly sunny and sometimes almost mild, as in very early springtime. And every morning now, the bluebirds come back to the nest box where they raised their babies last summer. They pop their heads in and out through the doorway, and often the female climbs all the way inside while the male sits on the roof to keep watch. If she stays too long, he clambers down, too, to hang in the doorway. He pokes his head in like the impatient spouse he apparently is. I don't know if he's worried for her safety or merely curious about what's taking so long in there.

I'm a bit surprised to see them because of all the ruckus that has erupted nearby. Yet another builder has torn down a house and is putting up a huge new one in its place, taller than any other on our street. There is a constant hammering and sawing, an endless procession of giant trucks coming and going, grinding their gears and beeping. Radios broadcast music all day long, and the carpenters sing at the tops of their voices as they fling heavy two-by-six boards straight up to each other, floor by floor. When the workmen leave at the end of the day, the crows come to investigate, stalking along the roof beams and peering into the scaffolding. The bluebirds ignore them all, crows and workers alike.

Unperturbed, they come every afternoon to eat the mealworms they know I will put out for them toward evening, and every morning they return with the parade of construction vehicles to explore the nest box they know so well. They look for all the world as though they, too, are planning for the future, setting things in order for babies to arrive once winter is past.

What they are actually doing is reasserting ownership of the box. Instead of roosting in trees on bitter nights, whole families of bluebirds will gather in a nest box or tree cavity to conserve body heat and take shelter from the elements.

"But this is where we raised our babies," I whisper to Haywood at night.

It is our endless conversation, now that the last of our parents is gone, now that our children are grown. We don't need all these rooms. We are tired of the noise and the traffic and the pollution of this growing city. We can hardly find our way around it anymore, so lost are the landmarks that once told us where we were. Two of our closest friends have made plans to leave when they retire, and two others have already bought the land they'll build on out of state. What if we found a cabin of our own in the woods somewhere not too far away? What if we downsized the house and upsized the yard?

But I tear up at the very thought of leaving this house full of memories, this neighborhood full of friends. I think of the baby nestled on my shoulder as I rocked him, patting his warm back, and the toddler who climbed into our bed after a bad dream, and the little boy teetering on a two-wheeler while Haywood ran beside him, jubilant. "You're doing it!" he would call as our boy wobbled beyond his reach. "Don't look down!" I think of the neighbors whose children grew up with ours. For all these years we have fed each other's dogs and watered each other's tomatoes and seen each other through terrible struggles: illness and infertility and postpartum depression and divorce and troubled teens and dying parents and, most devastating of all, the loss of a child. It is far too late to forge such ties in a new place.

I think, too, of my wild neighbors. What would happen to the butterflies and the red wasps and the patient skink who suns herself on our stoop? What would become of the shy rat snake and the cranky mole who makes our yard a welcome landing place for wildflower seeds? Who would leave out pans of water on hot summer nights for raccoons and opossums and red foxes to drink from?

"I don't think I can leave," I say in the dark. "How could we ever leave?" I am trying not to cry.

"It's OK," Haywood whispers back, pulling me closer.

Every day I stand at my window and watch the bluebirds, and then I look past them to the cheerful competence of the human builders clinging to the scaffolding of the house that is taking shape under their hands. Standing before the sun-filled window of my own warm house, I can't help wondering what springtime will bring. I am far from feeling any confidence in the future, but when I look at the busy tableau before me, something flutters inside— something that feels just a little bit like hope.

This is the one world, bound to itself and exultant.

—ANNIE DILLARD, *Holy the Firm*

Author's Note

Although the narrative of *The Comfort of Crows* unfolds within the span of a single year, this book actually took several years to write. During that time, my life changed in some of the ways a human life almost inevitably will. My children grew up. The last of my elders died. I grew older myself. Much of what happens within the human realm—the emptying nest, the building of a stock-tank pond, and so on—took place during 2022, and I write about those events in the present tense. When I refer to human events that happened earlier than that, I have used the past tense.

That's not true for the essays that describe only the life unfolding in my backyard or in the woods surrounding the cabin on the bluff. I experience my own life as a linear narrative, as days pile upon days, but I experience the life of the natural world as a repeating pattern. Though written during different years, these are observations of nature in all its repetitions, unwinding according to the rhythm of the ages. Songbirds build nests; baby birds grow up (or don't); trees bud and then bloom; blossoms ripen into berries. Creatures from many branches of Earth's family tree arrive to feed on them all. From one year to the next, the wheel of life turns, and then turns again.

Nevertheless, it is a calamitous mistake in the Anthropocene to trust that flowers blooming in springtime and birds singing at dawn are a sign that all is right with the natural world. In truth, very little is right with the natural world, even on my half-acre lot in Tennessee. Every year now, animals and plants respond in heartbreaking ways to the devastation wrought by climate change, to the heedless growth of a burgeoning city. Winter is punctuated by warm spells that aren't due for months. Droughts burden every summer, and so do brutal flooding rains, a marriage of contradictions that belies everything we once knew about the seasons. These changes, too, repeat from year to year, but this pattern is not a wheel. It is Yeats's widening gyre. Its center cannot hold.

I rejoice in what is eternal, even as I force myself to face what is not, to let my heart be broken again and again and again. The very least I owe my wild neighbors is a willingness to witness their struggle, to compensate for their losses in every way I can, and to speak on their behalf about all the ways I can't. It is my dearest hope that you will do the same for your own wild neighbors. Rejoice and grieve. Do your best to help. Bear witness when you can't. Remember the crows, who tell us that we belong to one another, and to them.

Author's Acknowledgments

I have read enough books to know that hiking a wilderness trail can be a life-changing adventure. Other books have taught me that tending a small plot of land is also an adventure—quieter and gentler but equally life-changing.

The Comfort of Crows owes its shape not only to the breviaries and religious devotionals whose purpose it emulates and expands but also to books that trace the workings of the nearby natural world as it unfolds across a single year: Annie Dillard's *Pilgrim at Tinker Creek*, David George Haskell's *The Forest Unseen*, Sue Hubbell's *A Country Year*, Verlyn Klinkenborg's *The Rural Life*, Aldo Leopold's *A Sand County Almanac*. Though the ecosystems they chronicle may bear little resemblance to the first-ring suburbs, these writers demonstrate the importance of paying attention to a changing landscape, especially to humble terrains that too often escape the attention of everybody else. I am grateful for their testimony.

When you live in the same place for decades, the inhabitants of your backyard become your neighbors, and your human neighbors become your friends. I give thanks to all the dear friends who helped us raise our children—far more than the crows and the bluebirds, they are the reason why we stay.

In making this account of a backyard year, I have hewed to an expansive definition of *yard*, including not just my own half acre but also the trails at Radnor Lake State Natural Area, Warner Parks, and Nashville's extensive greenway system. In a city where the human world presses ever closer, these green spaces grow more indispensable with each new high-rise, each newly widened road. They are urgently needed, and they are not enough.

One backyard that is as dear to me as our own is the forest that surrounds a tiny cabin on a cloud-drenched bluff overlooking Lost Cove. Rod and Jennie Murray created this haven by moving an ancient family cabin in Kentucky and rebuilding it, log by log, at the very edge of the Cumberland Plateau. They have been careful guardians of the land and generous friends to us. *The Comfort of Crows* would not exist if not for the peace of that quiet place. Even more than the gift of its sanctuary, I am thankful for the gift of the Murrays' friendship.

Several of these essays, or portions of them, first appeared in the opinion pages of the *New York Times*. For this book I have revised them significantly, often radically and unrecognizably. As always, I am grateful to Kathleen Kingsbury, Patrick Healy, Vanessa Mobley, and Ariel Kaminer for the opportunity to write about the subjects—and the creatures—dearest to my heart. I am especially indebted to my editor, Peter Catapano, for his compassionate guidance, his innate sense of pacing, and his unerring eye for the salient detail. I waited a professional lifetime for the chance to work with Peter, and every week I am reminded of how lucky I am that my essays landed on his desk at last.

In one of the greatest bits of luck ever to befall me, my first book came under the editorial guidance of Joey McGarvey, who can somehow take a sheaf of individual essays and find the central thread that unites them. She has found that elusive center for three books now, gently helping me to shape a whole out of many jagged parts. I am unendingly grateful to her—and to Cindy Spiegel, Julie Grau, and the whole team at Spiegel & Grau—for seeing this book into the world.

The literary ecosystem can be as intricate and inscrutable as any estuary or forest, and I am fortunate that my guide through its wildness is Kristyn Keene Benton. I have been the beneficiary of both her patience and her fierceness, and even more of her constant encouragement and support.

I am equally lucky that Ann Patchett built her now-legendary bookstore in my town. Parnassus Books, run by the brilliant Andy Brennan and his brilliant staff, is a corner of heaven for local readers and an entire cheerleading team for local writers.

The best thing that could happen to an author is to form a writing group with kindred souls who are both kind and exacting. Maria Browning and Mary Laura Philpott read every essay as I wrote it, read them all again in revision, and then *again* as a book. And the whole time their own beautiful writing gave me a model to aspire to.

Along with our parents, my brother and sister were my very first inspirations. Billy and Lori remain my inspiration, but now they are joined by my husband and children and longtime friends. The family I was born into, the family I chose, the family I created—they have been the making of me as a human being and as a writer. I give thanks to God for them every day.

Artist's Acknowledgments

For so many seasons together, about a hundred and twenty of them so far, I am grateful to my beloved, Susan Hicks Bryant. I was an artist before I met Susan, but I had not yet learned to think about color, and her influence is always with me as I work.

I am also grateful to my friends Mark Magnuson and Steve Westfield, whose retreat in the woods kept me in tune for this project during the last year.

Finally, I am grateful to my friend Greg Sand: his keen eye and careful work are invaluable in the studio.

About the Author

Margaret Renkl is the author of *Graceland, At Last: Notes on Hope and Heartache From the American South* and *Late Migrations: A Natural History of Love and Loss*. She is a contributing opinion writer for the *New York Times*, where her essays appear weekly. The founding editor of *Chapter 16*, a daily literary publication of Humanities Tennessee, and a graduate of Auburn University and the University of South Carolina, she lives in Nashville.

About the Artist

Billy Renkl is an artist whose work has been featured in many solo and group exhibitions, including shows in Nashville, New Orleans, New York City, Cincinnati, and Berlin, Germany. He is the illustrator of *Late Migrations: A Natural History of Love and Loss* by Margaret Renkl and *When You Breathe* by Diana Farid, among other projects. Renkl is a graduate of Auburn University and the University of South Carolina. He lives in Clarksville, Tennessee, where he teaches at Austin Peay State University.